Learning for Leadership

Other titles of related interest published by Karnac Books

LEARNING FOR LEADERSHIP

INTERPERSONAL AND INTERGROUP RELATIONS

by

A. K. Rice

KARNAC BOOKS

London

First published in 1965 by Tavistock Publications Limited.

This edition published in 1999 by

H. Karnac (Books) Ltd.

58 Gloucester Road

London SW7 4QY

by arrangement with The Tavistock Institute

Copyright © 1965 The Tavistock Institute

British Library cataloguing in Publication Data

A C.I.P. record for this book is available from the British Library.

ISBN 1 85575 233 6

10 9 8 7 6 5 4 3 2 1

Contents

Figures

Acknowledgements

This book is a personal account of what has been essentially a collaborative piece of work. My deep gratitude is due to all my colleagues on the staffs of the various conferences and courses I have directed. Their names are listed in the appendix. I must also thank the many men and women who have attended the conferences and courses as members. Without them none of the events described here would have been possible.

The Rowntree Memorial Trust made two generous grants to the early conferences. Out of them bursaries were awarded to members other than those from industry and commerce who would otherwise have been unable to attend. The trustees' understanding and support of a new and untried venture were of tremendous value and encouragement to us all. Funds made available to the Tavistock Institute by W. G. Ellis have provided bursaries for the courses held in London, and the Tavistock Institute of Medical Psychology has also provided bursaries for one course in London and for advanced training at the 1965 conference.

I should like to pay a special tribute to John Allaway of the University of Leicester. His courage and imagination, particularly through the early, difficult years of the growth and development of the conferences run jointly by the University and the Tavistock Institute, were of enormous support to us all. I should also like to acknowledge my deep debt to my colleagues Isabel Menzies and Pierre Turquet for their major contributions to the thinking and planning of both conferences and courses.

In the last two joint conferences Pierre Turquet has helped to design and operate the new events we have introduced. I am especially grateful not only for his own contributions but for the loyalty he has given me personally. Without it, the role I have taken would have been intolerable.

I know that all my colleagues on the staff and members of the conferences and courses would wish me to express their deep gratitude to Daphne Bostock, the conference secretary. She gives herself unsparingly and unselfishly to her job. I often wonder if my colleagues and I appreciate sufficiently how much her concern and care for individuals free us to think about and to experiment with technical innovations. I know that I myself owe her a debt that cannot adequately be repaid.

Many of my colleagues have read a draft of the book. I am very grateful for their constructive comments and suggestions. Eric Miller in particular not only commented on the draft, and made many suggestions for revision, but has also worked on the revised version.

Finally, I should like to thank Fiona Hunter Russell, Irene Davis, and other members of the Institute Secretarial Staff for their patience and care in typing the drafts and the manuscript.

3 *Devonshire Street*   A.K.R.
*London W.*1   *August* 1964

PART I

Conacrence Design

CHAPTERS

CHAPTER 1

Introduction

An account of the first full-scale experiment in the laboratory method of training in group relations in the United Kingdom was given by my colleagues E. L. Trist and C. Sofer (1959). They described the conference, organized by the University of Leicester and the Tavistock Institute of Human Relations, held in September 1957. Since that first conference, seven more have been organized jointly by the Institute and the University of Leicester, other conferences and courses have been run by the Institute alone, and still others by the Institute in collaboration with other bodies. I was a member of the staff of the first conference and of three out of four of those held between 1959 and 1961. I have been the director of the last three run jointly with the University of Leicester, of one conference run by the Institute, and of two shorter experimental conferences run in collaboration with Christian Teamwork.

The conferences have all been residential. In addition, I have directed two non-residential courses at the Institute. These have consisted of weekly events spread over six months. The programmes of the conferences and courses have been similar, but to avoid awkwardness in writing and confusion between them, I shall describe only the residential conferences in the early chapters of this book and reserve until a later chapter discussion about the differences between them and the non-residential courses.

This account is influenced by my experience of the early Leicester/Tavistock joint conferences of which I was a staff member, but it is written about the conferences and courses that I have directed. It is therefore a personal account given from a particular point of view. Though I was appointed director by my colleagues who have formed the conference staff, and though I continue to hold office only with their sanction, I have directed in my own way; and as director I have been in a privileged position when decisions about design and method have had to be made. My colleagues have not always agreed either with my approach to, or with my actions in, the conferences. But they have not disagreed so much as to

3

make our disagreements intolerable or their support impossible. They have influenced not only conference design but also my own conduct in more ways than I can make explicit or even know about. We still disagree on some points of theory and on more of practice. At this stage of our understanding of problems of interpersonal and intergroup relations, I believe it to be right and healthy that we should continue to differ, provided we can also continue to use our differences constructively.

This is not therefore an agreed account, and I have to accept responsibility for it. I am nevertheless writing it now because developments are continually taking place, and if we wait until we are all agreed about what we are doing and how we are trying to do it, I doubt if an account will ever be written.

This account, then, is intended as a personal contribution to a developing field. By its nature, it can be only a description of work in progress.

My introduction to this method of training in human relations was as organizer and then member of what I believe was the first civilian training group in the United Kingdom using non-directive methods. It was held in 1945. There were twelve members of the group when it started and three consultants to it.[1] For a variety or reasons that group was short-lived and at the end of six sessions was discontinued. I then became a member of a training group at the Tavistock Clinic, with W. R. Bion as its consultant. This group met at weekly intervals over a period of two years through 1947 and 1948. It was in size and method what we have since called a 'study group', and this is the term I shall use throughout this book. The study group is the equivalent of the 'T-groups' of training laboratories in both America and Europe though it tends to be smaller than the T-group. Mainly because of its cost, this specific kind of training activity in the Tavistock Institute and Clinic was suspended, and instead the Clinic concentrated on the development of group therapy and on other kinds of training for allied professional groups. It was revived at the 1957 conference.

In recent years there has been a growing body of literature about training in human relations and considerable research into its effectiveness.[2] Most of the research and the literature are American, though as this kind of training extends in Europe, so does inquiry into its techniques and their

[1] W. R. Bion, J. Rickman, and J. D. Sutherland.

[2] In particular, Argyris (1962); Bennis (1959); Burke and Bennis (1961); Bradford and Gibb (1964); National Training Laboratory (1953); Tannenbaum, Weschler, and Massarik (1961); Weschler and Schein (1962).

4

results. One difficulty has been, and is, to integrate this kind of training into more traditional academic courses in the behavioural sciences and into the fast-growing field of management education. In both, what Tibble has called the compartmentalization of education[1] tends to separate subjects and to lead to the use of small groups and syndicates for teaching and training, with too little regard for the whole of which they are a part. One consequence has been that most research work has concentrated on the effectiveness of parts of the training, usually of the study groups or T-groups. There has been less work on defining the task and nature of the training institution as an institution in its own right, and on the part played in it by the various events that it comprises. Thus the names given to conferences and courses, by ourselves as well as by others – 'group relations laboratories', 'human relations seminars', 'sensitivity training courses', 'conferences in interpersonal and intergroup relations' – have, on the whole, been more descriptive of content than of purpose.

I am now working on the assumption that the primary task of the residential conferences with which my colleagues and I are concerned is to provide those who attend with opportunities to learn about leadership. Leadership involves sensitivity to the feelings and attitudes of others, ability to understand what is happening in a group at the unconscious as well as the conscious level, and skill in acting in ways that contribute to, rather than hinder, task performance. But increased sensitivity and understanding are means, not ends, and the end is the production of more effective leaders and followers.[2]

Men and women in managerial, professional, or administrative roles – in industry and commerce, education, the medical and social services, and government – always have to work in and with groups of other men and women. Most now recognize that they cannot ignore individual or group needs and sentiments when making the decisions through which they dis-

1 Tibble, J. W. 'Learning'. A lecture given at Leicester/Tavistock conferences, 1963 /1964.

2 In this context, 'leadership' is used in its most general sense. The concept is discussed more fully in the next chapter. Thus a manager issuing orders for some task performance is leading, or trying to lead, his subordinates; but he is also 'leading' when he is acting in such a way that by his behaviour he is, consciously or unconsciously, setting an example. Again, a shop steward arguing with management is taking a lead on behalf of his members, even when, as sometimes happens, they disown him and his actions (Rice, 1951). Equally, a doctor is exercising a form of leadership when he tries to cure a patient or a group of patients; and a teacher is leading a class when he is trying to get his students to learn something.

charge their responsibilities and exercise their authority. They are depressingly aware how often many otherwise well-conceived plans fail because of unforeseen or, if foreseen, unmodifiable, resistance to change; how they become uncertain when under pressure; how they so frequently fail to communicate the genuineness of their intentions to superiors, colleagues, or subordinates; and how elaborate communications systems so frequently appear to break down. They are also aware that good intentions and common sense are not always sufficiently reliable guides for dealing with the resistance, or indeed for making judgements about either its strength or its validity.

In recent years there has been increasing understanding of the behaviour of individuals and of groups. But knowing about group processes and human behaviour does not necessarily mean that use can be made of the knowledge and understanding. Moreover, knowledge, let alone its effective use, cannot generally be gained from reading, lectures, or seminars. Both the acquisition of knowledge and learning how to use it require direct experience. The aim of the conferences described here is therefore to enable the members to learn, through direct experience, how to work with others as individuals and as members of the groups to which they belong. The conferences provide opportunities for members to experience what forces are brought to bear on them when they take roles that require them to lead others, and what forces they bring to bear on those who lead them. They learn what it feels like to be, and how to behave as, both leader and follower, and they experience the conflicts that arise in themselves and in others when they take these roles.

The assumption I make is not only that this experience is valuable for any leader or follower, but that it is the essential common element in the training of any manager, whatever kind of operation he manages, and whatever his status. The techniques of management – the kinds of organization required, the control mechanisms used, and the criteria for judgement of performance – vary according to what has to be managed. In some institutions, as in industry and commerce, results can be measured with some precision, at least in the long run; in other areas – education, medicine, and the social services – neither criteria nor techniques are so easily defined. These differences affect the relationships between superiors and subordinates, between colleagues, between professional workers, and between them and their clients; they must also affect transactions and communications across the boundaries that divide organizations from other organizations and parts of one organization from its other parts.

6

But all managers, administrators, and professional workers, in whatever field they work, have to use more than techniques; as a minimum they have to come to terms with themselves, and with the personal and group characteristics of those who man the institutions in which they work. To be successful they have to make constructive use of their own personalities. Members of a board of directors of a public company have to come to terms with their shareholders, with banks and investors, with government departments and trade unions, with their suppliers and customers, their managers and workers, as well as with each other; their managers may be protected from some of these complexities but they too have to make multiple relationships. Teachers in schools, universities, and training colleges have to deal with their pupils and the families of their pupils, their professional superiors, government both local and national, their trade union, and their colleagues. The catalogue is almost endless for every job or role, but making a relationship with each person or group in the catalogue demands an understanding of the personal, group, and institutional forces that determine the kinds of transaction that are possible. Few men and women are not called upon, at some time in their careers, to take leadership roles of some kind. Whenever they do so, they are inevitably the focus of conflicting forces that they have to reconcile as best they can.

Between the first and the more recent conferences there have been many changes in design and programme. Not all of these have been retained, and in general the principles on which the first conference was designed have, for the most part, been reaffirmed. Two new events have been added: one, the study of intergroup relations; the other, the study of the behaviour of the large group. An intergroup exercise was first introduced at a conference held towards the end of 1959 (Higgin and Bridger, 1964). In the conferences to be described here this exercise has been retained, but in a different form. The study of the behaviour of the large group is the most recent addition. In the early training groups and conferences 'the central feature . . . . is the creation of small groups which undertake the task of self study. These groups themselves act as laboratories for direct observation and analysis of social and psychological processes. With the help of a professional consultant and observer, such a group examines its own behaviour in an endeavour to find out what is happening in the "here and now", in the field of its own relationships' (Allaway, 1959). This method of study has now been extended to intergroup processes and to large as well as small groups. Leaders, in whatever field or at whatever level they operate, have always to deal with more than their own intimates.

They have to deal with groups that are larger than face-to-face groups; and on behalf of both small and large groups, they have to deal with other individuals, and with other small and large groups in their environment. Though in the conferences the study of small-group behaviour still appears to have considerable impact, it is no longer such a central feature, and its relative importance has thereby been reduced.

Some events of the original conference have now been discarded. These changes and the reasons for them are discussed later. The most significant change, however, has been the more conscious use both of the conference itself as an institution and of the processes of conference management in order to enhance the learning experiences for both members and staff.

The report of the first conference (Trist and Sofer, 1959) was an account of work in progress – so is this. I hope that readers will find that the concepts behind conference design are more articulate than they were when we started, and that the accounts of practice show that we have now realized some at least of the implications of that first experimental design.

The book is divided into three parts. In the remainder of this part the concepts and assumptions behind conference design are stated, and the resulting conference structure and culture described. Part II examines the conference events. Part III contrasts concentrated residential conferences and non-residential courses spread over time, discusses the role of director and relations within the staff group, takes up problems of training for staff membership, considers differences between training and therapy, and finally suggests a programme of research work.

The appendix gives the names of the members of staff of all the conferences and courses I have directed since 1962, to all of whom I am deeply indebted.

CHAPTER 2

The Basis of Conference Design

One event in these conferences is a lecture series, in which we try, among other things, to make explicit the main theories on which the design of the conference is based. My object in this chapter is to summarize the concepts and assumptions that are particularly relevant to the more detailed descriptions of the conference and its events in the subsequent chapters.

They fall into five categories. First, there are the concepts to describe human behaviour, and here I concentrate on those aspects of individual, small-group, and large-group behaviour that are usually latent in everyday working life. Events in the conference are designed, we hope, to allow members to become more aware of, and learn how to deal with, these latent aspects. In the second category are the theories of organization that are relevant to the design of the conference as an educational institution. Third, since it is in their various roles as leaders that members will apply what they may learn, it is necessary to say something about our concept of leadership. Fourth, I touch briefly on learning theory, with special emphasis on the problems of learning directly from experience – 'knowledge-of-acquaintance' – in contrast to more intellectual kinds of learning. Finally, and also briefly, I discuss the basic staff role in helping members to learn from the experience provided in the conferences.

THE INDIVIDUAL, THE SMALL GROUP, AND THE LARGE GROUP

The assumption that is made throughout the book is that individual behaviour is affected by unconscious forces, and, as a corollary, that individuals and groups of individuals always behave in ways that are not wholly explicable in terms of their rational and overt intentions. It is also assumed that, in any group or institution, unconscious motives affect the decisions that are taken; that any committee meeting, for example, has both a written and an unwritten agenda and it is the unwritten agenda

9

that takes up much of the time; and that jealousies, guilt, anxiety, and undisclosed and often unrecognized struggles for power have a profound effect on the acceptance or rejection of solutions to apparently straightforward problems. In short, it is assumed that intelligent human beings, whether acting alone or as members of groups, do not behave stupidly or in ways that are manifestly opposed to their declared interests without cause; and that understanding of the denied or repressed causes can make a major contribution to the solution of problems of leadership.

The Individual

The personality of the individual is made up of his biological inheritance and the experiences through which he passes, particularly those of early infancy and childhood. In a modern industrial society ordinary men and women have three overlapping areas of conduct – family, work, and social activities – through which they can work out their own development. Through these areas of conduct they satisfy their physiological and psychological needs and defend themselves against the stresses and strains of having to come to terms with the realities of their environment. They grow to maturity through the relationships they make in them. A baby is dependent on one person – his mother. He gradually assimilates into his pattern of relationships his father and any siblings. As he grows into childhood he includes other members of the extended family and of the family network. The first break with this family pattern is usually made when the child goes to school and encounters for the first time an institution to which he has to contribute as a member of a wider society. It is his first experience of what, in later years, will be a working environment.

The hopes and fears that govern the individual's expectations of the way he will be treated by others and the beliefs and attitudes on which he bases his code of conduct derive from these relationships and are built into the pattern that becomes his personality. They form his internal world. This contains his primitive inborn impulses, and the primitive controls over them that derive from his earliest relationships with authority usually represented by his mother and father. His internal world embodies that part of himself that longs to do what was forbidden or made impossible, and that part that is composed of the images of those who both excited, and forbade, the impulses.

A useful contribution to our understanding of the development of personality is made by object-relations theory. According to this theory, the baby can make no distinction between what is inside himself and what is outside. He has no 'ego' that can differentiate his feelings and their causes. What he feels about an object that is outside becomes an attribute of the object itself. He 'projects' his feeling onto it. So far as it excites him and gratifies him, it is a 'good object' which he loves and on which he lavishes his care; so far as it frustrates or hurts him, it is a 'bad object' which he hates and on which he vents his rage. In his struggle to deal with these contradictory attributes he splits objects into good and bad, which represent their satisfying and frustrating aspects. But, in reality, he has to learn that it is the same object that sometimes satisfies and sometimes frustrates, that is sometimes good and sometimes bad. Both what later appears as protective love and what appears as destructive hate may originate in one confused and violent feeling that is inherently unstable because, in his very need to take in what is good, the individual also takes in what is bad, and hence threatens to destroy what he wants most to preserve. From this violent confusion of feelings for the same object come the later tendencies, on the one hand, to idealize those who are felt to be protective and loving, and, on the other, to execrate those who are felt to be antagonistic and obstructive.

In the mature individual, the ego – the concept of the self as a unique individual – mediates the relationships between the internal world of good and bad objects and the external world of reality, and thus takes, in relation to the personality, a 'leadership' role. The mature ego is one that can differentiate between what is real in the outside world and what is projected onto it from the inside, what should be accepted and incorporated into experience and what should be rejected. In short, the mature ego is one that can define the boundary between what is inside and what is outside, and can control the transactions between the one and the other.

The tendency for most human beings to split the good from the bad in themselves and to project their resultant feelings upon others is one of the major barriers to the understanding and control of behaviour. And the difficulties of accepting that love and hatred can be felt for the same person are intensified in the relations between leaders and followers. Followers depend on their leaders to identify their goal, to devise ways of reaching it, and to lead towards it. A leader who fails, or even falters, as inevitably he sometimes must, deprives his followers of satisfaction and hence earns their hatred. But leadership is a lonely role and leaders must have followers; any hanging back or turning away is a threat to their own fulfilment. This inevitable, and mutual, dependence increases the need of both leaders and followers to defend themselves against the destructive power of their potential hostility to each other. Any attempt to study and to learn about leadership must therefore take account of this inherent hostility, and an understanding of its source and its nature must be a part of any learning.

The Small Group

By 'small group' is meant the 'primary' or 'face-to-face' group. It must consist of more than one individual, and it must not contain more members than can sustain continuous and close personal relationships. The accepted number varies with different cultures. But, in most, the relationships that have to be sustained in groups with more than twelve to fifteen members become so complex that the group tends to split into subgroups. In the conferences and courses described here, twelve is the maximum number that is used for small-group learning.

There is an extensive literature on small-group characteristics and behaviour. I am concerned here with those aspects of group behaviour that arise from the unconscious forces contributed by the group members. A major contribution to the understanding of these forces has been made by Bion (1961). He has suggested that a group always behaves simultaneously at two levels. At the manifest level a group meets to perform a specific task; at the same time it behaves as if it had made one of three discrete assumptions: to reproduce itself; to obtain security from one individual upon whom its members can depend; or to preserve itself by attacking someone or something, or by running away. He distinguished these characteristics of group life as the *work group*, the group met to perform its specific task; and the *basic group*, the group acting on one of the discrete assumptions. The basic group met to reproduce itself he called *pairing*; the group met to obtain security from one person, *dependent*, and the group met to fight or to run away, *fight-flight*.[1]

A basic assumption is a tacit assumption; and members of a group behave *as if* they were aware of it, even though it is unconscious. Not only is participation in a basic assumption unavoidable, but it involves each member's sharing in the emotions to which he contributes. Bion postulated that the individual member of a group is affected disagreeably whenever he thinks or behaves in a manner at variance with the prevailing assumption.

1 My own experience in groups, which started when I was a member of a Bion training group, makes me feel that pairing and dependence are, like fight-flight, opposite poles of the same assumption. The dependent group has met to obtain security from an individual who can never satisfy the demands made on him; the pairing group in the hope of producing the new magical dependent leader, a hope that is always vain.

In a group behaving simultaneously as a work group and as a basic group, conflict is therefore found between:

(a) the basic group and the individuals who compose it;
(b) the work group and the basic group;
(c) the work group suffused with the emotions associated with one basic assumption and the other repressed or denied basic assumptions.

The more a group manages to maintain a sophisticated level of behaviour, the more it uses the emotions associated with one basic assumption to suppress and control the emotions associated with the other two. Thus for a group involved in a fight the appropriate assumption that should be mobilized is 'fight-flight', and the group uses this assumption to suppress and control 'pairing' and 'dependence'. But if casualties mount the group may no longer be able to suppress the emotions associated with either reproduction or security, and its members may lose their stomach for the fight and the basic assumption may change.

The 'internal world' of the small group is made up, then, of the contributions of its members to its work task and to its basic assumptions. At the level of task performance members take part as rational mature human beings; at the level of the basic assumption they go into an unconscious collusion that may support or resist performance of their manifest task. The resulting pattern of interpersonal relations is therefore one of cooperation and conflict between the members of the group as individuals and between them and the group culture they produce. The external environment of the group includes other individuals, groups, and institutions with which the group, as a group, has relationships. Leadership, however transient and changing, is required to control transactions between the group and its environment. If the prevailing basic assumption is appropriate to task performance, the work leader may also lead the basic group; but if the basic group is in conflict with the work group, a different internal leader may be required to give expression to the emotions associated with the prevailing assumption.

The Large Group

The large group is defined simply as one in which face-to-face relationships are no longer possible. It is composed of individuals and of small groups, who may or may not be organized formally. Whether or not there is a formal structure, the members of a large group will also be grouped informally in static or changing patterns. The internal life of the

13

large group consists therefore of the relationships between individuals, and of the relationships within and between the small groups to which they belong. Individuals have their own needs and unconscious motives, and the small groups their tasks and basic assumptions. Without a formal structure to define its task, its boundaries, and its role system, the large group is thus the victim of confused individual strivings and small-group assumptions. If the same basic assumption prevails simultaneously in all the small groups that compose a large group, the attitudes and feelings associated with the assumption are powerfully reinforced. In such circumstances appeals to reason, to thought before action, have little chance of success. The group moves impulsively and with compelling force. If different basic assumptions prevail in different parts of the large group, small-group membership can change with bewildering rapidity as individuals try to join up with those in unconscious collusion with themselves. The resulting pattern is one of confusion, inaction, futility, and frustration. In this condition an individual who can define some positive goal can exercise powerful leadership.

The external environment of the large group consists of other individuals, and of small and large groups. It also consists, however, of its own members in other roles and as members of other groups. Leadership of the large group is thus required to control the internal and confused strivings of its members and to relate them to the external environment. Without a clearly defined purpose and boundaries that determine who is inside and who is outside – without structure – the large group is at the mercy of the most strongly expressed primitive impulses.

The pattern of individual, small group, and large group is shown diagrammatically in *Figure 1*. In this diagram:

p	=	the internal world of the individual, comprised of whole and part objects dynamically related to each other
P	=	the leadership function exercised by the ego
E_P	=	the external environment of the individual
g	=	the internal world of the small group made up of its interpersonal relations
G	=	leadership of the work group
E_G	=	the external environment of the small group
l	=	the internal world of the large group composed of its interpersonal and intergroup relations
L	=	leadership of the large group
E_L	=	the external environment of the large group.

FIGURE 1 *Diagrammatic representation of relations between individual, small–group, and large–group organizations*

THE INDIVIDUAL

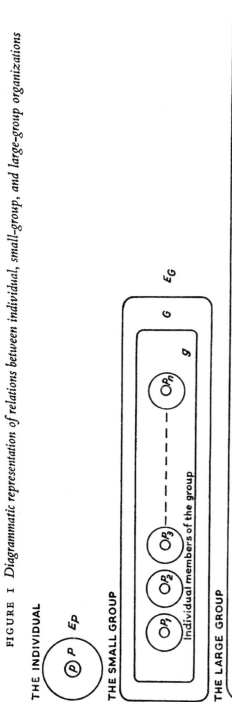

THE SMALL GROUP

THE LARGE GROUP

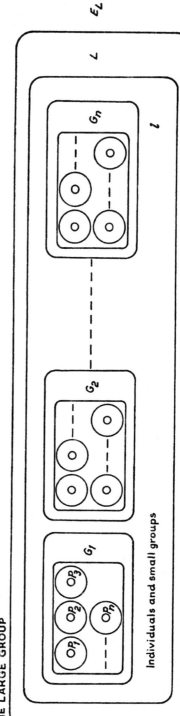

By organization is meant a set of administrative arrangements to cope with a given task. In this sense, individuals and groups have 'organizations' which may be more or less disorganized.

E, the external environment, is always composite, and includes, for individuals and groups, other individuals and groups. Moreover, each *P* can be a member of more than one small group in any large group and of more than one large group in any environment.

The roles taken by the individual in the internal life of the small group are examined in study groups; the internal life of the large group is examined in the large-group event; and small- and large-group leadership in the intergroup exercise and in plenary sessions. With each increase in complexity, new dimensions have to be taken into account. Thus, in the study group only what is happening in that small group is relevant. In the large group not only its own internal life but the interpersonal relations in its subgroups as they form and dissolve have to be studied. In the intergroup exercise the interpersonal life of small groups and the relations between small groups in the large group intrude on the building of suitable organizations for studying intergroup relations. The techniques used and their relevance to the various tasks are discussed in subsequent chapters.

Any examination of group behaviour, whether of a small or a large group, has to take account not only of the individuals involved, and of their personal and role relationships, but also of the expectations and beliefs they bring to the situation from the culture to which they belong. In an organized group the structure requires that its members take specific roles, and the formal structure comprises the system of roles so designed. Structure and roles are usually felt by the individual to be external to himself, as something 'out there', and it is by the process of taking up a role or roles in a structure that an individual becomes a member of the group. The nature of the social structure lays down the formal relationships between roles. The implication of a formal role relationship is that a person taking a particular role must establish relationships with other specified individuals occupying related roles, not as a matter of choice, but through the demands of the social structure. To roles are attached responsibilities and authorities, and role relationships determine the official communications possible between members of a group. The pattern of roles and of relationships gives the formal setting in which behaviour occurs. Any member joining a group imports into it his expectations of structures and roles and their attributes that he has acquired in his day-to-day life.

But groups of all sizes, as well as individuals, develop their own 'identities', and behave at both conscious and unconscious levels. Attitudes and beliefs of groups about themselves, and about others outside, are determined not only by the rational discussions and decisions taken within the group but also by the unconscious beliefs and assumptions on which the group works. Hence the behaviour of any group is determined not only by what its members bring to it but also by the culture they develop in the group and the interaction of this culture with their previous expectations.

THE PRIMARY TASK AND THE ORGANIZATION MODEL[1]

In this section I propose to describe the concept of the primary task and a theory of organization based on open-system theory. I have found these useful in the analysis of many different kinds of institution, and particularly relevant to the design of conferences and courses about problems of leadership.

The Primary Task

Institutions perform many tasks simultaneously. Industrial and commercial enterprises, for example, purchase raw materials; manufacture, sell, and distribute products; provide employment; look after their employees; conduct research work; keep accounts; make profits and losses; and pay taxes and dividends. Educational institutions train students; purchase and use teaching equipment; maintain buildings; pay rates and taxes; provide opportunities for growth and jobs for teachers; and some award diplomas, degrees, and certificates to mark student proficiency. All institutions provide mechanisms at both conscious and unconscious levels for the satisfaction of human need and for defence against anxiety.

The number and distribution of tasks vary between and within institutions and over time. Each whole or part has, at any given time, *a primary task – the task it must perform if it is to survive.*

The overall primary task of industrial enterprises is to make profits; that of educational institutions is to provide opportunities for learning; and therapeutic institutions must cure at least some of their sick. Their primary tasks differ, and hence the information on which decisions are made, and the criteria for the judgement of their performance also differ.

Primary tasks can be defined with varying precision; the more precise the definition, the greater the constraints on task performance. Thus 'to

[1] Rice (1963).

provide opportunities for learning' applies to any educational institution; and a decision to teach particular subjects or a particular age group puts constraints on the methods that can be used, on the criteria for selection of students, and on the qualifications required of the staff. Every subsequent decision adds further constraints on definition and performance. Equally, few tasks can be performed in isolation. The environment in which they are performed also imposes constraints on what can be done and how it can be done. The general constraints are political, economic, legal, and social; the more particular constraints are the human and physical, scientific and technological resources available for performance.

All institutions may perform many tasks at the same time; but in some there is no settled order of priority. Such institutions can have no one primary task but several tasks, each of which may be primary at any one time. In a teaching hospital, for example, two tasks may be defined – to train medical students and to care for patients – both of which are essential for the survival of the institution. In the operating theatre, indeed, task priority may change from moment to moment, depending on the course of the operation.

Moreover, each part of a complex institution has its own distinct primary task, which differentiates it from other parts and from the whole, and each contributes to the primary task of the whole. But the contributions are not necessarily equal, and can be in conflict.

The primary task of the conferences that are the subject of this book is to provide opportunities for members to learn about leadership. The methods of performance are:

(a) to provide members with opportunities to experience for themselves the interpersonal and intergroup relationships involved in leadership, in situations in which the experience can be turned into learning;

(b) to teach theories that offer verbal explanations of the learning;

(c) to provide opportunities for members to consider the application of conference learning to their normal work situations.

Each part of the conference, therefore, has its own primary task, which is different from the tasks of other parts but is designed to contribute to the primary task of the whole. The problem of conference design is to achieve this integration, and at the same time provide opportunity to experience and study any conflicts (and some are inevitable) between the primary tasks of the parts and of the whole.

The Organization Model

If organization is a means to an end, and the end is primary task performance, then it follows that the most appropriate organization for any institution, or part of it, is that giving a best fit to primary task performance.

Any institution considered as an open system can be defined by its imports and exports; that is, by the manifestation of its relations with its environment. The basic model that is used to design the organization of the conference is an import-conversion-export model derived from open-system theory. The assumption is made that the organization of any enterprise or institution, or parts of it, can be accommodated to this basic model.

Conferences have many imports: members who come from different jobs in different enterprises; staff from a variety of institutions; equipment; housing; food and drink. They also have many exports: members and staff returning to their ordinary work; payments for board, lodging, and other services; papers, brochures, and this book. But the dominant import-conversion-export process, by which the primary task of the conference is performed, is the process by which members enter the conference, go through its events (taking or not taking the opportunities provided), and finally leave it.

A model for the organization of a whole institution must of necessity take account of the differences in the primary tasks of the parts, and since these primary tasks differ, their organizations may also have to differ. Ideally, of course, the sum of the parts adds up to the whole, but ideals are seldom realized in human affairs, and compromise between organization and task and between the organizations of the different parts is frequently the only practical solution. What is important is that the need for compromise should be thoroughly tested. Thus a desirable timing of conference events may conflict with the housing or feeding arrangements of the centre in which the conference is held, or the accommodation available may conflict with its desirable allocation for various activities. So far as is possible, the organizations required for housing, feeding, and social activities are subordinated to the organization required for learning about interpersonal and intergroup relations, and hence about leadership.

There are, of course, other constraints on primary task performance that result in compromise in design and organization. Time is limited and costs are high, and other constraints have been adumbrated. Not least are the human, scientific, and technical resources available for running con-

19

ferences of this kind. Even if we had more time for research and development, there would still be the constraint imposed by our inability to find solutions to the many problems posed by the task itself.

The dominant import-conversion-export process that determines the conference organization is shown in *Figure 2*.

LEADERSHIP

I find difficulty in differentiating between management and leadership. At the manifest level of behaviour a leader has to be able to carry his followers with him, inspire them, make decisions on their behalf, with or without their collaboration, and communicate the decisions to others; he has to be able to act in ways that will not only further task performance but enlist the cooperation of his followers by mobilizing the appropriate basic assumption. A manager has to get the best results out of the resources he has available or can make available – money, time, materials, and people. Both leaders and managers have to deal with different numbers of followers and subordinates, extending all the way from the small intimate face-to-face group of immediate colleagues to extended commands and even crowds.

To be successful, a manager has to display qualities of leadership and use techniques of management appropriate to the task of the group he is managing. Nevertheless, some leaders are clearly better at inspiring their followers and at leading institutions than they are at managing them; some managers are better managers, in the sense that they apply management techniques effectively, than they are inspirational leaders. Some leaders and managers are better with small groups than with large; some leaders can inspire crowds but earn little respect from their immediate followers; and some managers are better at thinking out strategy than they are at implementing tactics. In other words, while leading is not necessarily synonymous with office-holding, and leading a small group is not the same as leading a large one, there can be no clear boundaries between leadership and management at the manifest level, or between the leadership of small groups and that of medium-sized or large groups. Any institution, or part of it, whose managers do not give leadership in primary task performance is in obvious difficulty. But leadership can also be exercised unconsciously, and at this level 'management', which for me has an essentially rational connotation, cannot be applied. In this sense, whatever the in-

20

FIGURE 2 *The dominant import–conversion–export process of the conference*

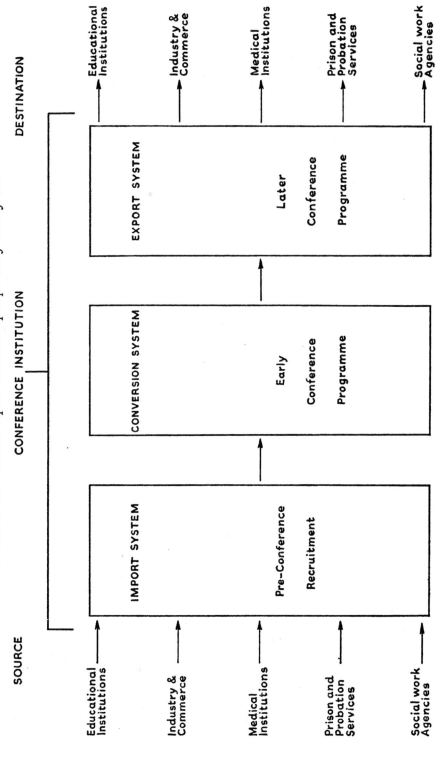

stitution, managers need to understand the problems of leadership, and particularly to be aware of those kinds of leadership, both manifest and covert, that oppose their management.

At the manifest level the primary task of leadership is to manage relations between an institution and its environment so as to permit optimal performance of the primary task of the institution. For an institution the environment consists of its total political, social, and economic surroundings; for a part of an institution the environment includes other parts and the whole. A task leader must define the primary task of the institution, or part of it, that he is leading, and keep under constant review both definition and constraints; he must recruit the necessary resources for performance, and control their use.

At the unconscious level the leader expresses, on behalf of the group, the emotions associated with the prevailing basic assumption. As I have tried to show earlier, he may or may not be the leader in the performance of the manifest task. His leadership is a function of the group and its internal strivings. He is less concerned with the declared and rational task of the group than with its emotional climate. In effect he is concerned with transactions across the internal boundaries of the group, that is, with its interpersonal relations. Thus, if the leader at the manifest level fails to deal adequately with the emotions associated with the repressed assumptions, other leaders may be thrown up to express emotions that are opposed to the overt task of the group, and hence to oppose the leader at the manifest level. The leaders of work groups should therefore have some understanding, however intuitive, of group processes, and be capable of mobilizing the assumption appropriate to the task, and to the situation in which it has to be performed. In a competitive industrial situation, for example, a leader must be able to mobilize 'fight' – and direct the fight against competitors. At the same time, he must be aware of the cost to his followers of all-out competition and provide the means by which those who cannot stand the pace are adequately helped to acquire new skills or are found other jobs, and, if found other jobs, are replaced by more competent successors.

When, in mature groups, there is a conflict between the group carrying out its manifest task and the group behaving as if it had made one of the basic assumptions, the leader in task performance is in danger of being rendered impotent by the conflicting demands made upon him. In these circumstances, other leaders may take some of the conflicting roles, even though at the manifest level no leader appears to receive full support. In

22

some work with a family business, one of the major problems my clients and I had to tackle was the conflict between the different kinds of leadership required. The father, who had virtually retired from business, was still the acknowledged head of the family. His son, who had taken over from him as chairman of the company, was the most powerful and competent member of the family in its commercial concerns, but business decisions that required shareholders' sanction were invariably made by his father. At the same time, a cousin in the business was also used, largely unconsciously, by the family to limit the authority given to the son. While deploring disagreements between the son and the cousin, the family always seemed to give just enough support to the cousin to make sure that he did not get so frustrated as to leave. At another level, family leadership was also exercised in different ways and in different directions by the female members of the family: their business interests were for the most part confined to the opportunities for management employment that would be provided for their children and to the funds they could obtain as a result of their shareholding. To provide family succession and financial security they insisted that the father, his son, and his nephew should agree about business management, however divergent their views. They thus imposed conditions that inhibited the full development of male leadership in either business or family. A still further complication was the leadership exercised from time to time by members of the family who could not be available for company meetings because of urgent family affairs. In Bion's terms, they were the leaders of the flight group, and their absence was used by the members present to avoid or at least postpone the painful process of making decisions that would have acknowledged the different aims of family and business.

LEARNING FROM EXPERIENCE

In the *Social Problems of an Industrial Civilization*, Mayo (1945) pointed to the difference between skill and knowledge. He emphasized that a science starts with the acquisition of a technical skill, and grows with skilled workers' attempts to make explicit the assumptions that are implicit in the skill itself: '. . . scientific abstractions are not drawn from thin air or uncontrolled reflection: they are from the beginning rooted deeply in a preexistent skill'. He refers to the important distinction made by William James between 'knowing about', the product of reflective and abstract thinking, and 'knowledge-of-acquaintance', which comes from direct experience of fact and situation. He quotes a letter from Alan Gregg: 'Knowledge derived from experience is hard to transmit, except by example, imitation and trial and error, whereas erudition (knowledge about) is easily put into symbols – words, graphs, maps. Now this means that skills, though transmissible to other persons, are only slowly so and never truly articulate.'

Two heroes die hard in our culture: the gifted amateur and the born leader. The hero of our educational system plays games well with little or no training, and gets first-class honours on the minimum of study. The great leader is independent of his environment or his followers. Scientific and technological advance has done something to destroy these myths. In recent years, in the West at least, introspection, the attempt to understand human motives, and even getting professional help to understand them, have become more acceptable, even fashionable. But it is doubtful if the pain and suffering associated with the experience of learning about oneself and about one's relations with others are yet generally accepted or acceptable. At least, most training for management or administration still tends to concentrate on techniques and to ignore the equally, if not more, important field of interpersonal and intergroup behaviour. And for learning about this, 'knowledge-of-acquaintance' is essential.

There is even some danger that the very fashionableness of 'human relations training' will itself lead to the attempt to develop such painless techniques that learning itself will be jeopardized. The mitigation of pain, however desirable, may, unless we are careful, become self-defeating because real learning will not occur, and the skill will not be acquired. Let me emphasize that I do not believe that the inevitable pain of learning about oneself or about one's relations with others has any value for its own sake. Nor do I believe that 'trainers' have any God-given right to impose suffering on their students. Rather I believe that the capacity of a 'trainer' is limited. In the field of human relations he can provide opportunities for learning; he can teach little or nothing. Those who come as students must have the chance of learning or not learning, as they wish, or at least of learning at their own pace. The process of learning is a process of 'internalization', of incorporating felt experience into the inner world of fantasy and reason. The individual has the right to determine how quickly this process should go. He will resist learning if the process makes him anxious or frightened or if the rewards are insufficient. But successful learning and resistance are cumulative, and learning can be a part of a readiness for change that is inherent in any growing and maturing organism.

In the conferences described here, the basic method of providing opportunities to learn is to construct situations in which the task given to the members is to study their own behaviour as it happens. In each situation so constructed one or more staff members apply themselves, so far as they are able, to facilitate that task to the exclusion of all others. Only staff roles and staff relationships are defined. No rules are laid down for members. They are free to make their own. The staff design the programme and set a pattern of behaviour, and by the programme and their own behaviour create an institution that gives protection to the members to experiment. In effect, four main 'boundary controls' are imposed: the total conference institution – visitors are admitted only under very special conditions, and no reports are ever made on individual members; the events – the primary task of each is defined, and one event is not allowed to overlap any other; staff roles – staff stay 'in role' and do not carry one into another; and time – events start and stop on time so that members know for how long the study of behaviour will last, and for how long staff will maintain particular roles.

But the definition of the task of the conference as the study of its own behaviour, and the absence of structure save for that of the staff, force members either to set up an 'organization' for themselves or to abandon the task. It is in the attempt to set up 'organizations' and in the taking of roles in them that members have the opportunity to experience for themselves the forces that are brought to bear on them when they take roles requiring leadership, and the forces they bring to bear on others who demand their following.

In the structured groups of everyday life, the specific roles and role relationships, the procedures, the recognized standards of behaviour, provide defences against the recognition of underlying processes. For conference members in their relationships with each other these defences have been removed. In short, the basic conference method is to construct situations in which the conventional defences against recognizing or acting on interpersonal and intergroup hostilities and rivalries are either removed or at least reduced. This permits examination of the forces at work. The method consists therefore of lowering the barriers to the expression of feeling, both friendly and hostile; of providing opportunities for a continuous check on one's own feelings, and for comparing them with those of others, about given situations. Or, to put it another way, it is to check fantasy against reality. It means that the anxiety of learning

25

is enhanced, and that therefore the ways in which anxiety is generated and controlled become part of the learning opportunity.

How the conference is designed, how it is managed, how competently the staff carry out their tasks are all parts of the situation in which learning can take place. Everything that happens in the conference, therefore, whether by design or accident, is material for study.

THE BASIC STAFF ROLE

A member of the staff, acting as consultant in any conference event, has his own conceptual frameworks within which he observes the behaviour in front of him, including his own. He also has his 'knowledge-of-acquaintance' from his own 'learning by experience'. But when he is at work as a consultant he is a person who, in Rickman's words, 'at the moment of his most creative endeavours, lets these disciplines sink into the background of his consciousness and senses the direction of a process or the degree of freedom in the organization of persons seeking his advice'.[1] In other words, he uses his own feelings to sense what is happening. He cannot observe with a detached objectivity that relieves him of the responsibility of taking account of what he is feeling himself. If he finds himself becoming embarrassed, anxious, angry, hurt, or pleased, he can ask himself why he is feeling what he is feeling, and can attempt to sort out what comes from within himself and what is being projected onto him by conference members. So far as he is sure that some of the feeling is being projected onto him and is not the result of some idiosyncrasy of his own personality, he can use himself as a measuring instrument – however rough and ready – to give him information about the meaning of behaviour, both consciously and unconsciously motivated. If he can then find an explanation of the projection in terms of the specific task set for that event, he can make an 'interpretation' about the behaviour of those present, including himself. The interpretation may be accepted, rejected, or ignored – but whichever it is, consultant and members are then faced by another piece of behaviour related to his intervention.

So far as he his able, the consultant is concerned only with what is happening 'here and now'. Anything that has happened anywhere else or even 'here' a short time ago is relevant only in so far as it is evidence of the situation at the moment at which he intervenes. In practice, no inter-

[1] Rickman (1951), quoted by Sofer (1961).

26

pretation is ever quite 'here and now', in the sense that speaking about it not only involves some delay, but changes the situation that gave rise to it. What the consultant is feeling, as he is feeling it, is what is relevant. If expressing the feeling changes it, then it is the changed feeling that becomes relevant. The skill of the consultant lies in his capacity to analyse – on a barely conscious intellectual framework – his feelings, and to express them in ways that will help the members of the group to understand their own feelings as they are experiencing them. But this does not mean that either the feelings, or the understanding of them, are necessarily conscious. Much of the communication and hence much of the learning take place at the unconscious and experiential level. Learning also takes place in post-conference reflection, and in the intuitive recognition of similar experiences in other situations at other times.

Hence the consultant's behaviour is as important for learning as what he says; perhaps more so, since the words he uses to describe his feelings are symbols, of greater or less abstraction, of the behaviour they represent.

In addition, in the conference the staff represent authority. Apart from the other roles they take as consultants and lecturers, collectively they represent conference management. The members inevitably project upon them their fantasies, fears, and doubts about authority and its power, and the analysis of this projection requires the analysis of the relationships among the staff themselves to distinguish what is intrinsic to the staff group and what is projected onto them by the members. Hence the authority relationships within the staff, and the way staff members conduct themselves individually and collectively, provide further 'here and now' learning opportunities. These phenomena and the part they play in the conference will be discussed in relation to the conference as a whole and to its events in subsequent chapters.

CHAPTER 3

ConExference Structure

The conference institution is made up of two major sub-systems: pre-conference recruitment – the import system which produces the members; and the conference programme – the conversion-export system through which those members who arrive pass on their way to becoming ex-members. Where the conversion process ends and the export process starts varies for different members. There is no clearly defined boundary between them and they cannot therefore be differentiated organizationally into discrete sub-systems.

PRE-CONFERENCE RECRUITMENT: THE IMPORT SYSTEM

The primary task of the import system is the production of conference members. In the framework of any one conference it is a discrete operating system in that, by the time the conference starts, its task has been accomplished. In the framework of successive conferences it is a continuing system, since inquiries are often carried over from conference to conference, and what happens at any one conference has effects on recruitment for subsequent ones. But with recruitment for a single conference as a frame of reference, imports are inquirers; conversion is the turning of inquirers either into members or into those who decide not to attend; and exports are therefore the members and non-members that result.

Task performance involves the publication and circulation of brochures and other forms of advertising, dealing with applications for places and with registration, sending out pre-conference information to those who become members, and interviewing prospective members. By these means inquirers become potential members and potential members become members. Recruitment of members entails booking accommodation, deciding at what stage to introduce waiting lists, and so on. The overt

28

manifestations of these processes are the rules about dates of registration and of payment, and the issuing of joining instructions.

The major unsolved problem is how to communicate to inquirers what the conference can achieve, and how to prepare them for what will happen to them if they become members. The better the solution to this problem, the greater the freedom of choice inquirers will have.

Over the past seven years we have tried different methods of communication: seeing each potential member individually, arranging meetings of groups of inquirers to discuss the conference, and writing about it. If what members say during the conference can be taken as a reliable guide, none of these methods has been very successful. While this failure can be construed as confirmation of the hypothesis that learning can be achieved only through experience, I hope that this book may provide a little more evidence on which to base judgements about participation.

THE PROGRAMME: THE CONVERSION-EXPORT PROCESSES

A conference programme consists of several different kinds of event, each organized in a series. The major series are study group, large group, intergroup exercise, application group, and lecture. In addition there is a plenary opening at the beginning of the conference, and plenary reviews towards the end. Residential conferences have usually lasted two weeks, though shorter ones of four and six days have been organized recently. The shorter conferences have had both fewer series and fewer events in each series. Non-residential courses have lasted for five or six months, two events taking place in a three-hour period once a week, with weekends for the intergroup exercise. Their programme has been essentially similar to that of the two-week conferences.

The progress of a member through the various series of events at the most recent conferences is shown in *Figure 3*. The corresponding programme is shown in *Figure 4*, in which it will be seen that some compromises have had to be made to accommodate meal-times and times for rest, recuperation, and social activities.

With the conference programme as the frame of reference, imports are members who actually arrive and, after the opening, are more or less committed to try to put the programme into effect; the conversion process takes place in the events through which members move; the exports are the members who withdraw either temporarily or permanently

FIGURE 3 *The conference programme as a process*

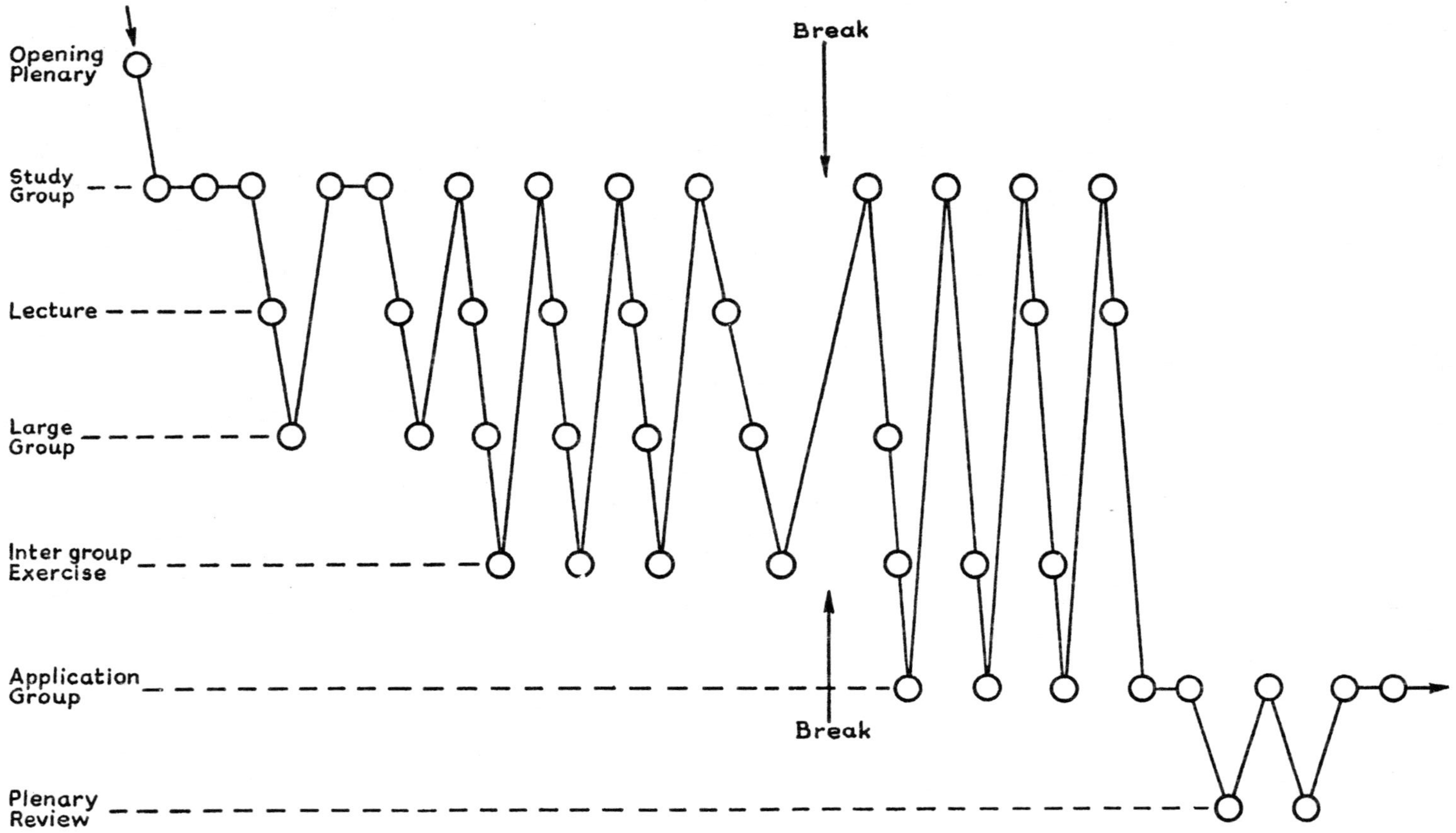

FIGURE 4 Conference programme

July 1964

Times	Wed. 15th	Thurs. 16th	Fri. 17th	Sat. 18th	Sun. 19th	Mon. 20th	Tues. 21st	Wed. 22nd	Thurs. 23rd	Fri. 24th	Sat. 25th	Sun. 26th	Mon. 27th	Tues. 28th
8.15 BREAKFAST														
9.0 – 10.30		SG	SG	SG	SG	SG	SG	—	—	SG	SG	SG	AG	AG
10.30 COFFEE														
11.0 – 12.15		Lect.	Lect.	Lect.	Lect.	Lect.	Lect.	—	SG	IGE	Lect.	Lect.	CR	AG
12.45 LUNCH														
2.15 – 3.45	CO (3.15)	—	—	—	—	—	LG	—	LG	—	—	—	—	
3.45 TEA														
4.15 – 5.45	SG	LG	LG	LG	LG	LG	IGE	—	IGE	AG	IGR	AG	AG	
6.30 DINNER														
7.30 – 9.0	SG	SG	—	IGE	IGE	IGE	—	—	AG	—	AG	—	CR	

AG = Application Group; CR = Conference Review; IGR = Intergroup Review; LG = Large Group; CO = Conference Opening; IGE = Intergroup Exercise; Lect. = Lecture; SG = Study Group.

before the end of the conference, and finally those who become ex-members at the end. Withdrawals before the end can be due to internal, personal, or group pressures; they can also be due to the intrusion of external reality.

Conference events are discussed more fully in subsequent chapters. Here I want only to place them in the context of the conference design and to discuss some of the reasons for their sequence and timing.

Members who arrive at a conference that is concerned with the interpersonal and intergroup relations involved in leadership are aware that this will involve their learning not only about others, but about themselves as well. They come to study their own and others' behaviour in a setting in which they know, or at least suspect, that many of the conventional defences against the expression and examination of feelings will be removed. They are therefore likely to be anxious. Verbal reassurance appears to be of little use in such a situation, and the conference is therefore designed to take members as quickly as possible into that series of events that experience has shown creates greatest anxiety. This is the series of study groups.

Study Groups

The task of the *study group* is to provide opportunities to learn about interpersonal relationships in small face-to-face groups. The primary task is therefore defined as the study of group behaviour in the 'here and now'. The object of study is what is happening at any given time; the aim is to match current feeling with contemporary experience. All assumptions about behaviour and beliefs on which behaviour is based are open for investigation. For this reason each study group is made up of individuals drawn from working and personal backgrounds that are as heterogeneous as the membership of the conference allows, so as to avoid, as far as possible, the importation into the group of conventions of behaviour from other common experiences. A study group consists of from eight to twelve members. That is, it is both large enough to enable individuals to relax from time to time without feeling that success in task performance depends on continuous effort, or that they are never out of the spotlight, and small enough to permit each member to maintain close personal relationships with all the other members.

A staff member acts as consultant to the study group. His task is to help the group to understand its own behaviour. He has no other authority. Members may attend the group or not as they wish, as indeed they may for any conference event; they may discuss and do what they like; the consultant alone is prescribed. He is there to try, so far as he is able, to interpret the group's behaviour to the group, and that of course includes his own contribution to it.

Because problems of interpersonal behaviour are examined and worked at in study groups, and because any form of group or intergroup activity impinges on interpersonal behaviour, the series of study groups has more events than any other in the conference and there is more overspill from it into other conference events. But because the study group is specially constructed to examine the underlying processes of small-group behaviour and has therefore no parallel in normal everyday life, the series stops before the end of the conference. In this sense the later meetings of the study groups can be said to prepare the way for the end of the conference, and hence to be a part of the export process.

The Large Group

The task of the *large group* is also to provide opportunities to learn about interpersonal relations as they happen, but in a setting in which the number of members is larger than can form a face-to-face group. The definition of its task is therefore the same as that of the study group: the difference lies in the constraints on task performance. In the large group, the individual not only faces all the other individuals, but he may also face major subgroups, in the form of study groups or other spontaneously created subgroups. He may himself seek anonymity in a subgroup or as a member of the whole.

The large group consists of the total conference membership, and two staff members act as consultants to it. As in the smaller study group, the consultants have no formal authority other than that of consultants. Whatever the group discusses or does, they must endeavour, so far as they can, to help the group to get on with the task as defined, and they should avoid, if they are able, going into collusion with the group to do anything else.

The series of large groups starts after some work has been done in study groups, since, in other situations than conferences, identification with the smaller working group usually precedes identification with the larger whole. The series stops before the end of the conference because, being composed of the total membership, it can have no continuing existence when the conference is over; it stops before the series of study groups to give opportunity in the study groups to deal with some of the inter-personal problems that the conflicting loyalties of the large group may have given rise to. In this sense the end of the large-group series marks the beginning of the conference export process.

The Intergroup Exercise

The task of the *intergroup exercise* is to study relationships between groups as they develop. Experience shows that as individual identification with a group grows, so conflict and rivalry between groups tend to intensify. At the same time there is increasing curiosity about members of other groups and about what other groups are doing. For these reasons, the intergroup exercise starts after some work has been done both in study groups and in the large group. As soon as an individual identifies himself as a member of any group he takes on a new kind of loyalty. And this raises questions about his previous loyalties. If he likes his new group, he may find he is beginning to dislike other groups; if he becomes worried about what his new group is doing or believes in, he begins to wish he could change to some other group.

By the time the intergroup exercise starts, members have already experienced, in study groups and in the large group, some of the difficulties of communication; for communication between groups a new complexity is added – representation. In other words, for a group to communicate with another group as a group rather than individuals, some way has to be found whereby its views can be represented. Some kind of political machinery has to be devised.

Among the members of a conference there are, of course, many possible groupings, depending on the criteria for membership and on the study groups that have already met. But within the conference institution there are two clearly definable groups – that of the members and that of the staff. The staff group already has its 'political' and administrative machinery, the members have none. In the intergroup exercise they are invited to divide up into groups in any way they wish, rooms are provided for meetings, and a given number of specified staff members are made available to those groups who ask for consultant help. If the members split into more groups, and if there are more requests for help, than there are staff available, some groups go without; if there are fewer groups, some staff members remain unemployed. The rest of the staff stay together in a room or space of their own and thus form a group for the exercise. They represent conference and exercise management.

Since the intergroup exercise involves the whole membership and the whole staff, it ends with a review at which all are present.

Lectures

A series of *lectures*, one of which is given on most days, is designed to give intellectual content to the learning taking place in other events of the conference. The lectures are intended to provide a framework for the articulation of the experience of the conference.

The lecture series has, however, an important secondary task: to provide a traditional form of teaching within a learning situation that is using unfamiliar methods. The hope is that the interpolation of a traditional method will have two effects: first, to provide some relief from the intense emotional experiences of other events – a working break; and second, to demonstrate a link between traditional teaching and the other methods used in the conference. Leadership does not consist only in understanding group processes; it requires as well an intellectual grasp of the problems of management, administration, and control. Learning about leadership has therefore to encompass all the techniques of learning.

The lecture series is in two parts. The first deals with theories of individual, small-group, and organized large-group behaviour; the second, which is shorter, with problems of learning and with examples of the application of the theories discussed earlier to practical work situations. Which particular examples are chosen depends upon the lecturers. They speak from their own experience.

Application Groups

The task of the *application group* is to consider the relevance of conference learning to normal work situations. For this reason members are divided into groups that are as homogeneous as possible so far as jobs are concerned. Groupings of prison governors, of general, sales, and production managers, of parish priests, personnel officers, training officers, heads of schools, training college staff, psychiatrists in private and institutional practice, psychologists and other kinds of specialist, are among the many that have occurred. The materials of discussion in the application group are 'cases' provided by the members. In contrast to the other events, excepting lectures, the learning is not about behaviour of the members in the 'here and now'; it is about past experience in other places, in the light of newly acquired experience and knowledge. All learning and teaching techniques are permissible: case conference, seminar, role-playing, led discussion, or any other method that is appropriate.

A member of the staff is attached to each application group. His duty is to help the group with its task. He is concerned with the 'here and now' of the application group only in so far as what is currently happening in the group interferes with its task. Even then, he uses his recognition of group process not necessarily to make comments on group behaviour but to help him to help the group to overcome the obstacles to its progress.

Application groups are started late in the programme so that members will have had some conference experience before coming to them and hence, it is hoped, will have some conference learning to apply. The conference ends with the application group because it is the series that is closest to everyday life, one that deals with the practical problems of members. In this sense the series of application groups is the real export process of the conference. In terms of the conference experience, members are by this time concerned with what they can take back with them. They have what they have, and have to accept it.

In addition to the events described above, two others are essential: the opening plenary and the closing reviews. And for conferences lasting two weeks we have always introduced a break of at least twenty-four hours midway through the period.

The Conference Opening
The *opening plenary* takes place as soon as the members have arrived. Its task is to provide a ritual, but meaningful, beginning. It is not expected that much can be said at this stage that will add to the literature that members have received before they arrive, at least not much that they can readily absorb. But they have by this time joined the conference and some event has to symbolize this implicit commitment to the conference aim. The staff are introduced at the opening plenary so that, as the members enter the events of the conference, they will be able to identify their

36

consultants and other staff. Additional administrative arrangements not already notified are announced, and there is a statement of the programme and some explanation of the design on which it is based.

This opening session, as can be seen from *Figure 4*, is short. The reason is that, though no bar is put on members' raising questions, experience has shown that very few are asked spontaneously. To stimulate a discussion at this stage of the conference would convey to members the message that the staff expected immediate participation. The purpose of the conference is to allow members to learn what they will, when they will, from the opportunities provided, and such a message would contravene this intention.

On past occasions, when more time was allowed, discussion after the director's opening seemed false and forced. Since we have redefined the task of the opening plenary, we have found that the few questions raised – never more than one or two at any opening – have been 'test-outs'. They have invariably implied doubts about administrative and management competence on the one hand, and about the reality of flexibility within a defined structure on the other. On every occasion, a direct answer has appeared to satisfy the members and there has been no supplementary. At that stage of the conference the test-out has been successfully handled and there have been no further questions.

Conference Reviews
The conference reviews have two purposes: one, the primary task, to allow members to discuss together, and with the staff if they wish, the experiences that have impressed them – favourably or unfavourably – with a view to crystallizing some of the learning that has taken place; the other, the secondary task, to provide an opportunity to learn about ending. The sessions, usually two, are both normal conference sessions, and hence longer than the opening.

The conference reviews, which take place in plenary sessions, also allow for a final manifestation of the conference as a whole. They are not, however, the final events of the conference. Application groups continue. The intention is to encourage both members and staff to work at trying to understand what has been happening and to concentrate on ending the conference without however applying closure to the learning process. The practice at the more familiar kinds of conference is to close with votes of thanks from members to staff for organizing the conference (whatever

37

they think of it) and to hosts for accommodation and catering (whatever their quality). The staff, in their turn, usually thank the members for attending and tell them what a good audience they have been. Convention decrees that whatever members may think of the staff, or staff of members for that matter, the closing ritual shall consist of an exchange of compliments. Since the purpose of the conferences described here has been throughout to examine the roots of behaviour and thus to question the attitudes and feelings that may lie behind such an exchange, it seems important that what happens at the plenary reviews should be consistent with that purpose. A conventional ritual, for convention's sake, would suggest a failure in conference learning.

Nevertheless, since the conference is a special kind of institution in which the normal social conventions of interpersonal and intergroup behaviour of everyday life are either removed or controlled, it seems essential that in the process of transition back to ordinary life some of the conventions should be re-established: the review sessions provide one such convention.

The Mid-conference Break

Members use the break in various ways: some stay in the conference centre; others visit in the neighbourhood; others return home; and some, when the break occurs on a weekday, return to their normal jobs.

The break is short so that the contrast between life in the conference and out of it is not unduly prolonged. But it is long enough to renew experience of the external world, as a counterbalance to the sense of unreality that might begin to creep into the conference itself. The break, in effect, is a rehearsal for the end. It has the advantage, shared by all rehearsals, that it is not a final performance. It also gives members the opportunity to absent themselves from the remainder of the conference if they so wish. In addition, of course, the break provides a welcome rest from the intensive work of the conference itself.

Follow-up

There is at present no follow-up event as such. Previous conferences included this event as a definite post-conference phase. It has been dropped until we can both be sure of our definition of its task and feel that we have a reasonable technique for performing it. Four possible purposes could be fulfilled by a follow-up: a meeting of an alumni association, a reassurance that something had been accomplished, 'closure', and further learning. The major constraints on any of these are time and hence cost. It has never been found possible to devote more than a weekend to the follow-up event.

A meeting of alumni could be – and indeed has been – a pleasant renewal of the relationships made at the conference. But since the task of the conference is learning for leadership and it is only a transitional institution, its primary task is not the making of permanent relationships. A meeting of alumni could not, therefore, rank as a primary task of a follow-up event. Nor does it seem appropriate to meet merely for re-assurance that we have together accomplished something in our two weeks of hard work. Who needs to be reassured – and about what? It is not certain. 'Closure' is equally unsatisfactory. There can never be any end to learning about human relations; any closure achieved could only be false and could be construed as a defence against further learning.

Hence, the only appropriate primary task that we can find for a follow-up event is further learning. In other words, the follow-up event would have to become an extension of the conference. Short of designing a different kind of conference with long intervals between various events, or series of events, a brief follow-up to what has been a fortnight's intensive work does not give adequate time for much further learning. Technically, we have no answer. This is not to say that conferences could not, or should not, be designed to take place in two or more parts with intervals between. Unless, however, such conferences formed part of a longer training programme they would present difficult organizational and administrative, as well as financial, problems. So far none has been attempted.

The only kind of follow-up has been the creation of an advanced training group at subsequent conferences. Membership of the advanced training group is, however, by special invitation for special purposes. These are discussed in Chapter 13, 'Institutional Reproduction'.

CONFERENCE MANAGEMENT ORGANIZATION

Some conference management – control, coordination, and service – is essential if the conference is to take place at all. The problem is to ensure, so far as is possible, that the methods of management and the behaviour of 'managers' are consistent with the conference task. And since the primary task of the conference is to provide opportunities for learning about leadership, or, in management terms, about interpersonal and intergroup relations in situations in which authority and responsibility are the subjects of study, it is inevitable that conference management becomes one subject of study. This means that management roles have to be described and their boundaries of responsibility and authority defined, in such ways as to encourage, or at least not actively discourage, examination.

Conference management has three tasks: first, to design and plan the conference; second, to implement the plan in the pre-conference phase; and third, to run the conference. Each of these managerial tasks is different. The first is the responsibility of the professional staff to whom it is delegated by the institution(s) responsible for organizing the conference. They bring to bear knowledge about learning and teaching as well as experience of previous conferences. 'Management' in this task consists of convening the necessary meetings and running them in such a way that decisions about design and staffing get taken. The model for this kind of activity is that of a group of colleagues with a chairman appointed by themselves.

The second task – getting out the brochures; receiving and dealing with inquiries, booking, and registration; organizing accommodation and sending out essential information – demands efficient administration. The model is that of a manager with the necessary subordinate staff.

If, in the design and planning phase, the staff could predict the course of every conference event, as well as the whole; and if, in pre-conference administration, they could lay down procedures for every administrative contingency, the management required at the conference itself would be minimal. The professional staff members would carry out the various events for which they were responsible, administration in the sense of coordination and control would be a 'service' function, and the staff group would be on the model of a group of colleagues with a chairman, as in the design and planning phase. But because the conference is about what it is about, prediction is impossible and contingencies or even emergencies always arise. The staff cannot always, as a group, act with either the speed or the decisiveness that the emergency demands. They become deeply involved in the events, and in the groups for which they are responsible, and cannot but lose some perspective on the conference as a whole, and hence on the indirect, as distinct from the direct, causes of the emergency. For this reason we have instituted the office of director.

In contrast to the earlier conferences in which the 'officers' of management included a chairman, a programme director, and joint conference secretaries, we have now defined only two 'officer' roles: director and secretary, both of whom are appointed by the institution(s) responsible for the conference, and explicitly accepted by the professional staff taking part in the conference. In the design and planning phase the director takes the role of chairman of the staff group; the secretary is secretary to the meeting. In the pre-conference phase the director acts as conference general manager, the staff group becomes advisory to be called on only if required, and the secretary acts as manager of the import system, taking responsibility for the actual operations involved. In the conference itself the director combines the roles of executive chairman and director; he is vested with authority, and carries the responsibility to act in what he believes to be the best interests of the members irrespective of previous decisions and roles. The secretary takes charge of all administrative arrangements, is in liaison with the staff who are providing accommodation for the conference, and 'looks after' the members in a practical way. The consequences of these changes of role, and hence of the pattern of management, will be discussed in a later chapter. The resulting management organization is shown in *Figure 5* (p. 42).

FIGURE 5 *Conference management organization in recruitment and programme phases*

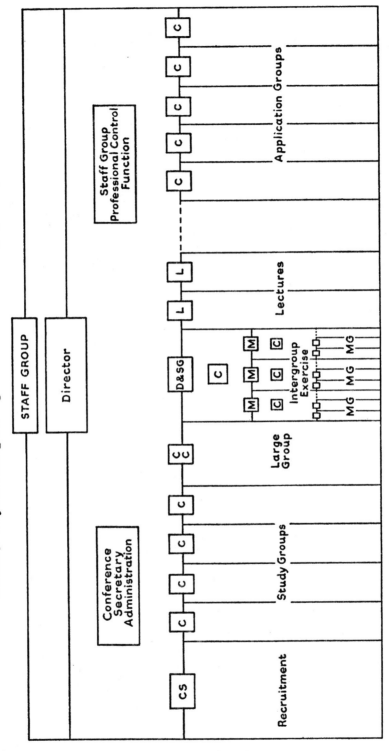

CS—Conference Secretary acting as manager in recruitment phase; C—Consultant; L—Lecturer; D & SG—Director of intergroup exercise and Staff Group remaining at 'centre'. M—Member-devised management; MG—Member Groups.

CHAPTER 4

Conference Culture

If learning about the real feelings underlying one's behaviour towards others and their behaviour to oneself can be painful and even distressing, then a conference that provides opportunities for such learning must provide some measure of security both for its members and for its staff. The basis of this protection is the way the conference is institutionalized. The structure of the conference institution – its design, formal organization, and management – has been described in the previous chapter. I shall now attempt to describe the kind of culture that we try to build up. The culture, together with the structure, forms the texture of the institution, gives it its 'life' within which individuals can exist and know something about where they are; can move and know something about whence they come and where they go. The culture of the conference is its customary and traditional ways of thinking and doing things, which, eventually, is shared to a greater or lesser degree by staff and members alike. It covers a wide range of behaviour – methods of work, skills and knowledge, attitudes towards authority and discipline, and the less conscious conventions and taboos. In any institution 'cultural congruence', the extent to which the culture 'fits' the task of the institution, is as important for effective task performance as structural fit.

Because of the nature of the conference, the culture has to be one in which aggressive behaviour, expressions of hostility between individuals and groups, can be studied and their effect on decision-making examined and learnt about, without their becoming destructive – either of the individual or of the conference. And since the task of the conference is to provide opportunities for learning about leadership, the pattern of authority and responsibility in the conference has to be sufficiently explicit to be capable of examination, and sufficiently stable to be able to tolerate critical and even hostile scrutiny. A culture that did not actively encourage such scrutiny would be incongruent, as would be one in which any particular conventional attitude towards human relationships became established.

43

The task of the conference is to provide opportunities to learn. How far members take the opportunities is their responsibility. Thus neither they nor the staff can predetermine how much part they will play in the life of the conference and hence in the building of its culture. At the beginning of the conference, therefore, it is conference management, conference setting, and staff behaviour that have to provide the means by which the basis of conference culture is established.

One other important protection for members is a conference setting that provides some degree of isolation from their normal working environment. It is for this reason that no reports of any kind – written or verbal – are ever made about members who attend conferences, no tests are given, no diplomas or other certificates awarded. In other words, so far as the staff are concerned, nothing that could be ascribed to any individual is ever disclosed outside the conference. Such protection, of course, can be no more than partial, since the staff cannot guarantee members' respect for confidentiality about each other. They can only set standards for themselves that they hope will be followed by members.

LEARNING ABOUT THE ANXIETY OF MAKING DECISIONS

Decision-making, the constant occupation of leadership, can frequently cause anxiety – anxiety about the amount and quality of information available on which the decision has to be based, anxiety about the capacity to make the decision, and anxiety after it has been made while waiting for its consequences. It is unlikely that much can be learned about anxiety without the learners themselves becoming anxious. The problem of the conference institution is not, therefore, to avoid anxiety, but to provide opportunities to examine its effect on behaviour and to learn ways of dealing with it, so that its outcome is constructive. The technical problem is to provide situations which, though they may provoke anxiety about behaviour and decision-making, yet still allow members to learn as much as they want to learn and at the rate at which they want to learn it. If a situation is actually worrying, then there is reality in worrying about it. The difficulty is to equate the nature and extent of the worry with the reality. Worrying about dangers that do not exist, or not worrying about dangers that do, are alike problems of testing reality against fantasy for the recognition and solution of which the conference exists.

But because the capacity to tolerate anxiety differs between individuals at different times and in different situations, it is inappropriate for one group at the conference, the staff, to try to teach another, the members, what to worry about, or to suggest that members should worry when they are not worrying or stop worrying when they are. The task is to provide members with the opportunities to learn, not to insist on their learning; but when they do want to take the opportunity provided, to help them to realize its potential.

Since one cannot learn much about anxiety without becoming anxious, members of staff who are not made anxious at some points in a conference are unlikely to be in close enough touch with what is happening in it to fill their own roles adequately. What is important is that the staff demonstrate that they can contain and understand their own anxieties and use them to further conference experience for the members; that is, that they can learn themselves from their own anxiety and through this provide opportunities for others to learn as well.

Furthermore, the staff must be able to cope with the kinds of situation they help to create. Even though they provide only opportunities for learning, and members must take their own responsibility for how much they learn, the provision of the opportunity itself implies that it is safe for members to take it. Moreover, members are not offered learning situations created by the staff alone; they are also subjected to situations created by other members, out of opportunities presented by the conference institution and the way it is run. The staff, therefore, cannot absolve themselves from responsibility for anything that occurs in the conference, whether inside or outside actual conference events. The capacity of the staff to take this responsibility lies not only in their individual abilities but in their collective skills organized in a conference institution to which, for a time at least, they have committed themselves.

It can be assumed that when members arrive at such a conference they are at least going to wonder what they have let themselves in for. They bring to the conference their own culture, with its expectations of 'structured' situations, of 'civilized' interpersonal and intergroup behaviour, of how leaders should behave under different conditions, of rules and procedures for regulating antisocial or deviant behaviour. They know from what they have read or heard, or from previous experience, that the techniques of conference learning include the removal of some of the common and expected social defences, the lowering of barriers to the expression of feeling, and an examination of the values that are placed on externally accepted modes of behaviour. Though they come willingly,

45

it is unlikely that they will be sure altogether that they have acted wisely. In that state, while most of them are strangers to each other, and before they have had an opportunity to experience just what a conference is like, they can only turn to the conference staff for help.

It is not the director's or the staff's job to reassure them, to tell them that there is nothing to worry about – there may be. Rather it is the staff's job to demonstrate that they know what they are doing and what they are not doing, to be prepared to tell members what they can do and what they cannot do, and to show that they can be depended upon to do what they say they are going to do. This, in Bion's terms, is a sophisticated use of the dependent basic assumption. At that stage, knowing nothing or very little about the actual experience they will encounter, members are, in reality, dependent: they depend on the staff for leadership. But if members are to accept staff leadership in this situation and to commit themselves to learn in such a conference institution then the staff must be demonstrably dependable. Knowledge of the job to be done, and a demonstration of competence, do not however mean omniscience and omnipotence, and the reality of staff dependability and the contrast between the knowledge and competence ascribed to them by members and how much they really know and how competent they really are will be tested during the course of the conference.

In short, the culture that we try to build is one in which, within a given framework, members will feel able to examine their own and others' behaviour in a series of settings that, while being specially constructed for the conference, throw light on the underlying processes of behaviour in common and familiar external situations.

CONFERENCE MANAGEMENT CULTURE

At the beginning of a conference different members accept or reject staff leadership in their own way. In varying degrees they accept the mores and customs of the institution they have entered, and in so doing add their own contribution to the conference culture. In this sense every conference is unique, but each is built on a type of management and a code of staff behaviour that are intended to provide an institution of sufficient stability to afford security, and of sufficient flexibility to permit members to experiment with different ways of tackling problems of leadership and followership.

For the members, the institutional framework is the programme of events, the roles taken by the staff, and the conference setting. No rules are laid down for them: they may attend events or not as they wish, and, within the constraints laid down by the place in which the conference is held, do as they wish.

So far as the staff are concerned, the programme is adhered to. Events start and stop at the published times. Members can arrive late or leave early; the staff stick to the plan laid down. This does not mean that the programme is inviolate. If something occurs that makes it desirable to vary the timing of an event, it can be changed. But it is important that the reasons for changing be adequate and real; that management is not led into making change for change's sake, to prove its own flexibility or its subscription to democratic principles. Because the discipline of time is imposed only on the staff, no bells are rung or other signals given to mark the beginnings of sessions; nobody shepherds the members into events.

In practice, the timekeeping at conferences has so far been remarkable. The usual pattern is for the members to be waiting for the staff. When no other conventional rituals are available, time can itself be used as a boundary control. Members accept timekeeping as a means of establishing their own discipline, of determining what is inside and what outside the boundary of an event. Inside, behaviour is under scrutiny and conventional defences are questioned; outside, normal social practice holds. As will be seen, timekeeping in the sense of staying until the programmed end of a session can also be used inside the boundary as a defence against further work. 'Sitting-it-out' can itself become a ritual.

As much factual information as possible is given to members before they arrive: the names of other members; their allocation to study and application groups; a plan of the buildings; where they will sleep, eat, and work; a list of amenities; and where possible the actual allocation of accommodation and workrooms. When they arrive their names are on the doors of the rooms they will occupy, and a conference office is open to deal with practical queries.

Name labels are not issued. The individual member is helped to get to know his surroundings by the information sent to him, and in the opening plenary he can identify the members of the staff with whom he will work. But he is not given artificial help to get to know other members, since the study of this process is a part of the conference content. Labels that identify name and organization – even when they can be read – are a conventional means of introduction at conferences. But the convention does not ensure personal contact; indeed, a label can be a defence against finding out what lies behind it. This defence is removed.

If the conference organization fits its task, the role designed for a member of the staff in any event is consistent with the task of the event. Events and roles then fit into a coherent whole. In consequence, the staff do not allow themselves, without good reason, to go into collusion with members to make un-thought-out or arbitrary variations in role or event. Of course, the fit is never as good as it should be; the authorities and responsibilities never match perfectly. The urge to make changes can therefore be very strong. And the more able and sophisticated the members, the more they can cloak their temptations as reasonable requests and thus inveigle staff out of role and away from the task. For, after all, the attempt to destroy authority and to make leadership impotent is one of the aspects of relationships between leaders and followers that the conference is called upon to study.

The more appropriate the conference organization is to its task of providing opportunities to learn about interpersonal and intergroup problems of leadership, the surer are those who operate the organization of their roles in it. The better they can stay in role, however many and various the roles they have to take, the greater the security members feel in an anxiety-provoking situation. Indeed, the demonstration that such aspects of human behaviour can be examined and discussed provides a framework in which members too can release for discussion data about themselves that they might otherwise be unwilling to release.

So far as is possible the conference structure defines the events, and the roles, responsibilities, and authorities of the staff in the various events in which they are engaged. The serious attempt to match the delegation of authority and responsibility, and to define the boundaries of events, puts severe constraints upon the staff. But there are compensations. Thus, though there may well be differences in technique and language among the staff who act as consultants to the study groups, the groups in the intergroup exercise, or the application groups, once they have been assigned their tasks, what they do and how they do it is up to them. Theoretically at least, staff are not assigned to conference roles unless they subscribe to the overall concept that has been worked out, but once they are appointed, they have not only the responsibility to implement that policy but the authority to do it in their own way.

The ability of the staff to take roles and to stick to them, to recognize the extent and the limits of the responsibility their roles carry, and to exercise authority within those limits are manifestations of their capacity to run the kind of conference they are running. This capacity, it is hoped, will encourage members to experiment themselves with different kinds of role-taking and with organizations of their own. They can then experience the kinds of responsibility they feel they can carry in different circumstances, and the amount of authority they can exercise.

STAFF BEHAVIOUR

Essentially, staff behaviour has to be 'professional'. By that I mean that members of the staff have to accept full responsibility for what they say and for how they behave. They have to know, usually without thinking about it, what is confidential and what is not, and to respect confidence without being secretive; they have to be able to differentiate between person and role, between task and personal needs, and to recognize when their personal feelings are affecting their role performance. They have also to be able to accept that they will never be paragons, and will inevitably be proved fallible; that making mistakes, as they will, is less important than the ability to recover from them. This means, in effect, that they strive always to remain in role, and that their behaviour, so far as they can control it, is appropriate to it.

In events they do what the event defines they should do; on social occasions they behave socially. They do not, if they can help it, merge the one with the other. This does not mean that at meals, in the bar, or on other social occasions they refuse to discuss the conference or its events if that is what interests those with whom they are talking – such behaviour would be antisocial. But it does mean that, outside conference events, their contributions to such discussions pay adequate regard to the confidential nature of the information at their disposal, and they avoid getting involved in additional 'extramural' events.

In 'public' events in which some members of the staff have no working role, as for example in a lecture, rules for staff behaviour are explicit. The primary task of a lecture is communication between the lecturer and the members. The 'platform' at such a session is therefore occupied by the lecturer or lecturers, and the body of the hall by those for whom the communication is intended – the members. Any staff who attend such a session, but are not on the platform, have therefore to regard themselves as being privileged visitors. They can participate in the discussion following the lecture only when they are certain that their contribution will help both 'platform' and 'hall'. It is inappropriate that they should intervene on either side to defend or to attack the lecturer. If staff not on the platform disagree with the lecturer, as can happen, the disagreement has to be dealt with privately, unless their comments would help lecturer as well as members. In other words, once the task of giving a lecture has been delegated to a lecturer, he has to be trusted to do it.

By contrast, in public events such as the conference opening, the plenary sessions of the intergroup exercise, and the conference reviews, those who are on the platform have not only the right but the obligation to do their best to help the members; and if this means shooting down the speaker in the interests of the members, then he has to be shot down. That is to say, open disagreement among the staff in front of members is appropriate if the disagreement furthers task performance. The judgement about task performance is not easy, and in practice public disagreement seldom occurs – the point is made to emphasize the insistence, in conference events, on the staff staying in role as far as they possibly can.

CONFERENCE SETTING

Conferences are usually held in colleges or the halls of residence of universities, occasionally in hotels. My own, and my colleagues', preference is for a university setting, which, though not necessarily as comfortable as a hotel, provides a working educational institution as a background. It is also cheaper. So far as the buildings used for conferences allow, all members have a room of their own, and three common rooms, apart from workrooms, are provided: one for members, one for staff, and the third (usually the bar) for both.

In a conference where the existence of different feelings for the same person – love and hate, like and dislike, trust and distrust – is accepted and where the hostility inherent in any human relationship is acknowledged, members need somewhere where they can let off steam privately and where they can collectively say exactly what they think about the staff. They need to be able to compare and contrast the behaviour and competence of different staff members, and to rehearse all the protests they want to make about conference organization, methods, and management. For this reason, their common room is inviolate to the staff. Once in their own common room, members can be assured that no member of the staff will be present by accident or design to overhear anything they may say.

In the same way, however, the staff too in their worry about the conference and about themselves want to be able to have not only technical discussions about what is happening and what they should do next, but also the opportunity to deal, in private, with their own anxieties, their own interpersonal conflicts, and their own feelings of inadequacy in the situations they have created. They also want to talk about the members. For this reason, they too have their own common room, which not only serves them as a workroom, but is also a place where they can relax, where their behaviour is on view only to one another and not to the members.

Given this segregation, it is easier for members and staff to meet in the bar over drinks, to mix in the dining room, and to talk about the conference or about anything else.

Not all places where conferences are held provide enough accommodation for workrooms, lecture rooms, and common rooms, and complete geographical separation is not always possible. In these settings, we have to make the separations by time. If an exclusive common room has to be used by staff and members for work, then for that time only is it declared not to be a common room. At all other times it is a common room to which common-room regulations apply.

In the same way, in conference events, the arrangement of the furniture represents, within the constraints of what is available, the structure of the event. Thus at the opening plenary and in the plenary reviews the total staff responsible for the conference are on the platform facing the members. At the plenary sessions of the intergroup exercise the different staff roles are represented by the grouping on the platform. In the large-group event there is no platform, the chairs being arranged in two, three, or more rings depending on the number present and the shape of the particular room. In the small-group events the arrangement of the chairs, the presence or absence of a table, are left to each individual consultant – and, of course, often become matters for discussion with the group.

In short, given the tasks of the total conference and of the events within it, as defined, we do the best we can to see that the roles and structures are appropriate to, and the culture congruent with, the task performance. The test we apply to any suggested change in design or arrangement is to what extent it fits task definition and what effect it might have on task performance.

PART II

Conterence Events

CHAPTER 5

Study Groups

In this and the succeeding chapters of Part II, I propose to discuss the major events of the conference. I am concerned more with content than with theory; not because I consider theory unimportant, but because each event would require a book on its own. Nevertheless, I hope to show that the different events do fit into a coherent whole that is consistent with a unified concept of human behaviour, however inadequately formulated.

I hope I have already shown in earlier chapters that any staff member responsible for an event has, by the nature of his task, only his own knowledge, experience, and feelings as his evidence for what is happening, and that these will arise from the relationships established within the group with which he is working. In my account of events, therefore, I can use as examples only my own experiences in them. Except in an emergency, and in one conference to be described later, I have not acted as consultant to a study group and as conference director at the same time. For this reason, to describe the study-group event I have to draw on material from other conferences than those that I have directed. I hope that my description will not be so atypical as to invalidate it for others.

In *Experiences in Groups*, Bion (1961) has described what happens in study groups to which he has acted as consultant. Sutherland (1959) has outlined the work of the study groups in the first Leicester/Tavistock conference in 1957. Many other writers, particularly in America, have written about this form of 'training' and the kind of insight it is intended to give. The techniques of 'taking' groups vary not only with consultants, or 'trainers' as they are called in America, but with the institutions in which the groups are 'taken'. There has also been much discussion about the differences and similarities between study groups and therapy groups, a question to which I shall return in Part III.

In this chapter I do not propose to argue for any particular technique or to suggest rules for the kind of 'interpretation' that should be, or can be, made by the consultant to a study group. I accept that each consultant will have his own insights and idiom of intervention. Provided that all consultants subscribe to the general theory of group behaviour on which the institution is based and genuinely try to help the groups to which they are attached, I make the assumption that when and how they intervene will not be of major importance.

I do not wish to imply that I think that all consultants are equally insightful or that all communicate their insight with equal clarity, but that, as yet, we are not able to differentiate between verbal and non-verbal communications, or between the task, structure, and personality variables that make up study-group behaviour to a sufficient extent to allow us to make conclusive judgements about either the words or the behaviour of consultants. A consultant makes a relationship with his study group – a relationship based on his own and their personalities. Within this relationship he does his job as best he can. Indeed, my own experience as consultant to a study group confirms my view that, as conference director, I have no option but to delegate fully both responsibility and authority to the consultants the staff group has chosen.

When, as consultant to a group, I make a comment on group behaviour that is immediately accepted as correct by all members of the group, I usually feel that my interpretation must have been so close to consciousness as to be of only small value in advancing the members' understanding of what is happening. Such acceptance is, of course, at first both gratifying and reassuring, but within a short time I cannot avoid feeling that the group has 'presented' me with material for an agreeable interpretation as a means of hiding more obscure behaviour which, if examined, would give rise to more painful feelings. If I make a comment which members immediately deny – often aggressively – only to behave subsequently as if they had accepted it, I feel the interpretation may have been of greater value. But often when I make an interpretation that is overtly ignored, I find that in the long run it turns out to have made a greater contribution to members' understanding of group processes than those that have been either accepted or denied. Nevertheless, even when I have been able to link interpretation and subsequent behaviour, my judgement of cause and effect may obviously be biased and I have no measurable answer to the charge that I have created my own findings and have set up a collusive system leading to self-fulfilling prophecies.

I propose to discuss the task of the study group, the usual pattern of behaviour that follows from this definition of the task, and how this task fits that of the conference.

THE PRIMARY TASK OF THE STUDY GROUP

The purpose of the study group is to 'provide an opportunity to learn about the interpersonal life of a group as it happens'. The group's task is therefore defined as the study of its own behaviour in the 'here and now'.

Members of study groups are selected from heterogeneous backgrounds. So far as is possible, the members of a group do not already know each other, nor do they know the consultant, nor do they do the same kind of job. The intention behind the heterogeneity is to avoid importing into the study group any of the conventions or traditions that are characteristic of a particular way of life, or any predetermined relationships that would, at least in the beginning, affect the life of the group. The intention, in short, is that members of the group should all start from scratch in getting to know each other and in building an interpersonal life. It is seldom possible today to compose study groups of complete strangers each from a different kind of job. Experience indeed suggests that heterogeneity is perhaps less important than we once thought it, and we, as well as others, have worked with groups of close colleagues (Argyris, 1962). However, in a short conference in which time for any one series of events is severely limited, the greater the differences of age, sex, and job among the members of a group, the easier it is for them to find common ground in the task they have been set.

The consultant's job is to help the group to study its own behaviour as a group. He is not concerned with individual behaviour as such, except in so far as it is a manifestation of group behaviour. By this I mean that the consultant is concerned with what the group is doing – how it is using its members to further its own ends, be it to work at its task or to avoid it. The consultant's leadership is task-orientated; he, if nobody else, must keep to the task defined.

Experience of conferences shows that what is to happen in study groups is usually the major preoccupation of most members on arrival. It is the event that causes them most anxiety. Until they have dealt with this anxiety by testing the reality of study-group experience against their fantasy of it, they find it difficult to pay much attention to other events. Moreover, on entering any new situation, most individuals try to find some small group with which they can identify themselves while they come to terms with their human and physical environment. For these reasons the first study-group session is timed to take place as soon after the opening of the conference as possible. The second and when possible the third sessions then precede the introduction of any other event. Equally, however, because study groups are constructed specially for the purpose of studying group behaviour and hence have few, if any, parallels in everyday life, they are stopped before the end of the conference.

DISCUSSION IN THE STUDY GROUP

In spite of all that has been written and said about study groups, most members appear surprised and even embarrassed when, at the beginning of the first session of the group, they find that the consultant does not behave like a traditional discussion group leader. In the opening plenary the consultant has been introduced by name to the conference; the task of the group and his role have been defined, and both have been described in the literature sent out in advance. Members nevertheless appear to expect some kind of introduction from him, even if it is only an announcement that the session should start.

Though there are, of course, individual variations, most consultants start as they intend to continue. That is, they study the behaviour of the group, which includes their own contribution to it, and intervene only when they think that their intervention will illuminate what they believe to be happening. They therefore seldom speak until they have some evidence of behaviour on which to base what they have to say. At the beginning of a series of study groups, they can have little or no evidence about the behaviour of the specific group. Hence, they remain silent.

At the first session of one study-group series the group, most of whose members had heard or read about consultant behaviour in study groups, arrived, more or less together, a few minutes before the session was due to begin. I arrived as the last members were going in, and went straight to one of the armchairs that I had previously arranged in a circle. There were two or three low tables in the circle on which ashtrays had been placed. There was a lively chatter as the members sat down, moved the tables to more convenient places, asking each other if they smoked, moved again to allow two friends to sit next to each other (it was not completely heterogeneous). Gradually, the chatter died down, until at the time the session was due to start there was complete silence. It was as though everyone had not only been looking at his watch (I did not observe anybody doing so), but had previously synchronized it with every other one. The members turned to me. I remained silent. After a few seconds, the member sitting on my right suggested that everybody should introduce himself.

He announced his name and the organization from which he came. He was followed by the member on his right, and so on round the group until the introductions finished with the member on my left. Before I could work out – and still less have time to say – what this meant in terms of group behaviour, in such a way that any comment I made could help the group to understand why it had ignored my non-participation in this way, two members started to discuss a particularly brutal murder that had taken place two days before, and was still front-page news in the daily press. Gradually, other members joined in, and the discussion, which was very serious, ranged over other similar crimes and on to capital punishment.

After fifteen minutes the discussion started to falter, contributions appeared to become forced, various attempts to revive the discussion by introducing new aspects of the incident and its implications were not taken up. Embarrassment grew, members found it difficult to look at each other, and started to look at me again. After about twenty minutes there was a silence and I made my first comment. I said that I felt that so far as the group was concerned I was the one who had been 'murdered', in that I had been prevented from getting on with my task. I pointed out that the group had been discussing an external event and had paid little attention to what was happening 'here and now', but that by their serious discussion they had made it difficult for me to intervene. I added that I felt that the faltering and embarrassment arose because members were feeling guilty about what they had done to me; but that they had done it to escape from the task they had met to perform. This comment was greeted with scorn and derision:

'We certainly haven't murdered you – what a way to talk!'

'I've never heard such nonsense. I'd just forgotten you were there.'

'You were perfectly free to join in the discussion.'

But I was not free to join in the discussion, except in so far as I believed that my contribution would be pertinent to the study of group behaviour. In Bion's terms, the prevailing assumption at the beginning was dependent; when I failed to take the role of leader of the dependent group, the member on my right stepped in; when that failed, a pair of members took over and the assumption was 'pairing', but the lead they gave produced 'flight'. My comment turned this into 'fight', with myself as the object of the hostility.

On another occasion at the start of a series of study groups the same lead was given – that is 'let us introduce ourselves' – but at the end of the introductions there was another awkward and embarrassed silence. And while I was wondering what to say:

'Well, we didn't learn much from that – in fact I've forgotten most of the names already. I seldom do pick them up the first time.'

So the members went round the group again, but not so systematically, asking each other questions: how to spell names, what each other's organizations did. This conversation died as the other had done, in embarrassed silence. Slapping his hands on the table (on this occasion we were in upright chairs round a table) a member said loudly:

'Well, that's cleared the decks!'

I commented that they had perhaps been cleared for a fight and that the fight was going to be against me for not doing what was expected of me – for not giving the kind of leadership they expected. I pointed to their hostility, shown by lack of support, to others who had tried to take a lead. The members individually and collectively denied they had any such feelings:

'*I* don't feel hostile, but I do feel afraid of what is going to happen. If only we had a clear purpose.'

'We need to establish formalities to enable us to discuss.'

'We're trying to find a common denominator. This is an unnatural situation. The trouble is that nothing is happening. There is nothing to study. We're not competing for a job or anything . . .(*a pause, in which tension in the group could be felt to mount*). We all look at Mr Rice . . . (*then another pause*). For God's sake somebody else talk!'

And the tension was broken by laughter.

Even though members have been told what their task is, they find the absence of the traditional leader, who will instruct them in how to tackle it – a task that is in reality difficult – worrying and even frightening. They feel as though they are being threatened by their lack of progress. Most groups struggle with this situation, and in the struggle seem able only to unite in hostility towards the consultant because he does little to relieve their distress. The assumption seems to be that he could help, if he would, and that it is only perversity on his part – or a trick, or manipulation – that stops him. He does not care enough for them, but when he suggests that they hate him for this:

'I don't understand what all this talk of hatred is about. I don't feel hatred for anybody here, not even for the consultant.'

'It's nonsense, I don't hate him, but I think he should speak more often. After all, he's paid to do that and we've paid to listen to him.'

Later these expressions modify:

'I don't understand all this talk of hatred and hostility, but I certainly get irritated with the way he keeps on harping on the subject. I'd forgotten he was here. I was interested in the topic.'

'He said he's not here to teach. I think he's here to enrich the Tavvy's experience.'

'Hell, I didn't pay for that!'

These exchanges lead usually to more overt discussion of 'leadership' and the qualities required of a leader. Invariably, the discussions become more abstract and intellectual:

'The leader has to personalize himself.'

'A leader has to be a man of integrity; he has to create an organization.'

'He has to see that the group gets on with its job, and provide the necessary equipment and knowledge to do it. If the group hasn't got it, it's his job to see that it is obtained.'

If the consultant intervenes, as he does, to suggest that it is his leadership that is found wanting, he is, in the early stages, either ignored or reassured. He is told that they are trying hard, but just have not got the knowledge. He is accused of holding back, or he is asked to elucidate some difficult point. Although it is not often said directly, he gets the impression that if only he would relent and give just a short dissertation on leadership, all would be well. Members show distress more openly, and when this happens others look at him with a 'There, see what you have done'. If he points out that the group is behaving as if it only had to produce a sufficiently moving case to make him try to do what he knows to be impossible, the group either gets angry with him or displays still more distress.

At some stage, particularly when he has prefaced some intervention

with 'I feel that . . .', he is brusquely told that his feelings are his own concern and that the group is not interested in them. As the sessions follow
each other, there is occasionally an attempt, usually short-lived, to create
a more familiar type of organization. Somebody suggests that a chairman
and a secretary should be appointed, agenda and minutes prepared. Only
one group that I have worked with has ever got to the point of electing
members to these roles, and on that occasion only one said that he would
accept office, but even he changed his mind before taking it:

'Don't we need a chairman to organize our discussions? He could bring
out people and keep order.'

'He could fertilize our discussion and direct it so that it doesn't wander.'

'I was scared stiff when you suggested me for chairman. I knew just
what you'd do to me if I accepted.'

'How do you mean "what we would do to you"?'

'You'd treat me as you've – I mean we've – treated Mr Rice, or anybody
else who has tried to get us to work at our job.'

With the failure of the members to sustain intellectual discussions either
of group problems in general or of leadership problems in particular, and
with their inability to arrive at any acceptable form of organization, there
frequently follows a period of depression and hopelessness. There is nothing to be learnt from this exercise: 'It is a waste of time' and 'It was a mis-
take to come' are common remarks. Members often deal with the depression by making jokes and by maintaining a strenuous belief that silences
are no longer disturbing:

'I visited the shrine of Cardinal Wolsey this afternoon.'

'Well, we're not interested.'

'Do psychiatrists put the price up when there is silence?'

'Would it be useful if I suggested . . .'

A chorus of 'No!'

'It's strange, but I don't find it nearly so difficult to tolerate silence as
I did at the beginning. I feel more at home with you all.'

And when one member who had been silent for an unusually long time
was asked why:

'I'm practising to be a consultant!'

Gradually, this kind of joking behaviour, interspersed with long and often discursive discussions about group process, about leadership in other situations, well-known leaders, religious conversions, the bringing up of children, usually leads to a more hopeful discussion about what has been learned: the toleration of silence, the relief at being able to express feelings more openly, the reassurance that their expression need not be destructive, that there is meaning in the study group:

> 'Let's list some of the things we've got from this group. For example, we know what we mean when we say a group fights or runs away; that it is dependent on its leader; that we let pairs try to find solutions for us; the group splits in different ways about different things, and different people take the lead, not necessarily those who should do. These very things happen back home in our boardrooms, departments, schools, and committees. If we have these things pointed out when we're experiencing them, they really mean something, they really come home.'

At this stage I am accepted, even praised, as the 'leader' who has brought this about. But this phase invariably takes place long before the end of the series. My refusal to go into collusion with the group in assessing how well it has done, and my interpretation of the 'stock-taking' as an attempt to escape the end of the group before the end has been reached, frequently lead, after denials, to a discussion of the techniques of running groups. If I go on to point out that the group appears to be assuming that, because we know that 'projection' takes place, we shall avoid it in future, the group tends to turn to an examination of my 'skill' in taking groups. If I then take this up as an attempt to make me once more into the 'good' leader, who will not let them go away empty-handed, there is either more joking or a further period of depression:

> 'What were we talking about that we were so keen to get on with?'
>
> (*Silence*)
>
> 'We were talking about why we attacked and ran away, and why we didn't seem able to control it.'
>
> (*Silence*)
>
> 'Something about groups and individuals who make them up.'
>
> (*Silence*)

And even irritation and anger seem useless. The depression comes from the realization that there is no escape from work if group behaviour is to be understood. A renewed attack on me or on the conference as a whole is normal, but by now the attacks are more sophisticated, and the inquiry into their origin and form is more deliberate and penetrating. Members who take a lead are not 'destroyed' so briskly and the reasons for dissatisfaction with their leadership are examined more closely. In one group a member said:

'I feel everything I thought I'd learnt has been useless; even what I thought I knew when I came seems of little value now,'

– and she burst into tears. But when other members of the group tried to comfort her and to reassure her that she was good at her job:

'Don't be such fools. I can at least cry here and look at why I'm crying.'

Not only is the group preoccupied with its ending, but feelings about it are the more intense because the group will finish before the end of the conference. By this time it is always difficult for members to accept the special nature of the study group and hence the reality of the need to finish it early; to acknowledge that it has only a limited value within the context of the conference. In this dilemma it is not unusual for members to say that the experience has been useless and has no value outside the conference setting, and that therefore the group can be disbanded without compunction or regret. But they find it difficult to accept that it can have been entirely useless when they have spent so much time in it. If, by contrast, they believe it to have been a wonderful experience, then it should not end before it has to, that is, at the end of the conference. Hence, its ending is either a major act of hostility on the part of the staff of which the consultant is a member, or the members have been misled by the staff into thinking the group would be more productive than it has been – and this too has been the consultant's fault for not making it better. Study groups usually end with members having feelings both of relief at the end of a trying experience and of regret and mourning for something valuable that has been lost. But if, mixed with these feelings, there can be some work at what ending means, then perhaps the study group has achieved its aim.

CONSULTANT TO A STUDY GROUP

Most members of study groups attend them to learn about what happens in groups. They know that this means the study of their own as well as of others' behaviour. They know that their own behaviour will be exposed to the scrutiny of the consultant and of their fellow members. They suspect that, though the consultant will not comment on them as individuals, what he says will refer to them and may imply criticism of their past behaviour.

In the group the consultant has only his own observations and feelings to guide him. He can feel worried, rejected, angry, confused, and embarrassed; or he can feel calm, wanted, happy, and relaxed. He can ask himself why he is feeling as he is feeling, and judge what arises from within himself as part of his own personality make-up and what comes from the group, what the group is projecting upon him. He can ask himself what these expressions of feeling mean in terms of group behaviour, and why the group is treating him in this way. If he can explain his feelings, and why they have arisen, he may then be able to help the group to understand its own behaviour.

Inherently, the members of any study group must at times feel hostile to their consultant. By becoming members of a study group and by accepting his role, they are consciously or unconsciously accepting that they need to understand more about their own behaviour towards others and about others' behaviour towards them. Inevitably they must hope that their learning will be largely about others, and that any change they may feel they have to make in their own behaviour will not reflect on themselves, but only suggest ways of accommodating to the foibles of others. But whatever the rationalization, unconsciously they have to accept that they might have failed in the past. This acceptance in itself, as it is realized, can be felt as an affront to their self-respect. They are not likely to let it go without challenge. The consultant's job is to confront the group, without affronting its members; to draw attention to group behaviour and not to individual behaviour; to point out how the group uses individuals to express its own emotions, how it exploits some members so that others can absolve themselves from the responsibility for such expression.

As a group fails to get its consultant to occupy the more traditional roles of teacher, seminar leader, or therapist, it will redouble its efforts until in desperation it will disown him and seek other leaders. When they too fail, they too will be disowned, often brutally. The group will then use its own brutality to try to get the consultant to change his task by eliciting his sympathy and care for those it has handled so roughly. If this manoeuvre fails, and it never completely fails, the group will tend to throw up other leaders to express its concern for its members and project its brutality onto the consultant. As rival leaders emerge it is the job of

65

the consultant, so far as he is able, to identify what the group is trying
to do and to explain it. His leadership is in task performance, and the task
is to understand what the group is doing 'now' and to explain why it is
doing it. Drawing attention to interesting phenomena without explanation is seldom useful.

THE STUDY GROUP IN THE CONFERENCE

The only overt constraints placed on the study group are the definition
of its task and the consultant's persistent attempt to refuse to do anything
else. Members can do what they like. They frequently ask:

'Why don't we go and watch a football match, or talk about racing?'

'Why don't we take a walk in the country?'

'Why do we even bother to sit in this room?'

Nothing but group pressures and their own conscience is stopping them
from doing anything they wish. No sanctions can be imposed. The only
discipline is imposed on the consultant, who will not, if he is able to avoid
it, go into collusion with the group to do anything other than study the
behaviour of the group, and that only for the time laid down in the programme. He 'controls the boundary' of the group, and thus provides
security for the members in three ways: he stays in role; he starts and
stops on time; and he maintains confidentiality.

In practice, members of study groups discuss almost anything from
leadership as an abstract concept to the kind of leadership they are getting
in their own group; from external events that have nothing whatever to
do with their task to their own feelings for each other. Gradually, during
the course of the conference, they learn that it is possible, in the study
group, to express their feelings more openly and frankly than is usual in
other groups; to question assumptions about value systems that it is
difficult, if not impossible, to question in more conventional settings;
and to build up a feeling of intimacy and security that here, in this group,
they can be themselves without fear of the consequences. This is what
usually gives rise to the euphoric feeling, part way through, of having
learnt so much.

The first crack in this euphoria comes with the realization that the group
will end, that death and coming to terms with it by adequate mourning

are an essential part of any living experience. Members realize that after the end of the conference some of them may meet each other again, but that the group, as a group, will not survive the conference. If it is so valuable then some means should be found of making it live on. The reality that it will not calls into question the process by which such intimacy and such reassurance have been achieved:

'I'd never have believed this kind of feeling was possible – but what is it? I feel I know you all well, and you me, but to what end? Haven't we really been fooled all along?'

'I'll be glad when this session is over. The first time I've really felt like this.'

'I think the (coffin) lid is down and screwed home, but are we right about the identity of the corpse?'

'It may be the consultant but I'm afraid it's the group.'

'It's going to be a difficult grave to arrange. Whoever lies next to . . . will have an uncomfortable time. He's bound to turn.'

'This feeling is as hard as a wall. Nobody dares to make a serious remark.'

'There's not much time. Why do we stay here to the bitter end? There's good clean air outside.'

In the study group members are face to face with a leadership that is neither destroyed by hatred nor rendered impotent by love. The consultant accepts a task responsibility and an authority that imposes no discipline on the members. He cannot impose any sanctions for failure to cooperate in task performance, nor, perhaps more importantly, can he reward good performance. Learning is its own reward; lack of learning its own punishment. It is for many members a new task, a new kind of authority, and a new kind of leadership, whose strength they can experience for themselves. They can defend it or attack it, imitate it or denounce it; they can learn from it.

The whole experience is within their grasp; nothing that happens outside the group is relevant to the task they have to perform. As a group they have no external environment to contend with; as individuals they have only each other and themselves. It is the most simple, and at the same time the most primitive and direct, experience of the forces that impinge on them when they lead and that they bring to bear on those who lead them.

In most conferences there are between twelve and fifteen study-group sessions, two or three of which take place before any other event is started. Thereafter members have to contend with an increasing number of different events. By contrast with experience of other events, study groups, when they are not in session, are frequently said to be warm and secure:

'You know where you are in a study group. You are intimate with everybody in it. It's safe to express your feelings there.'

Thus, in spite of its impact, it is one of the conference events that provide protection for experiment in other situations. It is for this reason that, though study groups finish before the end of the conference, they continue beyond the ending of other 'here and now' experiences. Ending them before the end of the whole is an attempt to ensure that if they have gained a false value – as comforting and secure – the test of the reality, the 'let down', is taken in the conference itself, while members are still there, and have the staff and each other to help them to cope.

CHAPTER 6

The Large-group Event

Many devices have been used to increase the participation of members in the events of conferences and training programmes. They have been developed in the hope and belief that participation, by reducing passive attendance, makes communication more effective. Small groups have always been used for training and learning. Since the Second World War many institutional conferences have adopted a pattern whereby speakers address the whole conference, and then discussion of the lectures takes place in small groups, which subsequently reassemble in plenary session to report back to the total membership. In 1947, at a conference run jointly by the Tavistock Institute and the Industrial Welfare Society, this technique was modified in that there were few speakers, and they only set themes, leaving the members to decide the content of the conference. Many variations are now common: in some, the small groups are given a specific question to discuss, either all the same question, or different ones for different groups; in others, usually the larger conferences, sections have their own speakers. 'Buzz' sessions (in which members form small units of from two to six persons without moving out of the conference room), role-playing, sociodrama, brains trusts, panel discussions, and debates are among techniques that have been used with success. Other conferences that have been concerned with understanding problems of human relationship and leadership have introduced forms of 'joint consultation' – committees composed of members and staff – in an attempt to reproduce, in the conference, the kind of relationship and leadership the conference has been advocating. All are attempts to establish organizational mechanisms that will allow an individual member to make his views heard without exposing him to the difficulty of addressing a large group.

Even in the small group it is not easy to expose one's feelings or to put forward ideas that have not been fully formulated, but at least the attempt can be made in an atmosphere of intimacy. In the small group as compared with the large group the individual is more likely to have a chance to explain himself without being made to feel guilty about taking more than a fair share of the available time, and to speak without feeling that he will be irrevocably committed to a point of view and have little or no opportunity of correcting himself. The large group provides a more public occasion, and the greater the number present, the greater the exposure. The large group therefore poses special problems for its members and its leaders. It demands different qualities of its leaders and different kinds of communication between its members if task performance is to be effective.

In the conferences I am describing the large-group event consists of a series of meetings of all members, together with two or more consultants from the staff. A large group, for conference purposes, is defined simply as one that is too large for face-to-face relationships. It is taken, literally, to be a group that cannot conveniently sit in one circle of a size that would allow members any hope of being able to make intimate relationships with the members opposite to them. In the large group, because of its size, some members have to sit behind others; hence a speaker can neither see nor be seen by everyone in the group.

There are, so far as we yet know, no specific limits on the numbers that should comprise a 'large group', though the characteristics displayed by groups of certain sizes will obviously preclude them from being studied in the way we have devised for use in conferences. My own experience, not only in conferences, but in industry, commerce, government service, and education, makes me feel that with up to six members a group changes in its characteristics with each additional member; that thereafter there is a different kind of change that differentiates a group of seven or more from one of less than seven. As the group grows from seven to eleven or twelve, other changes take place but without changing the essential characteristics of a small group. With over twelve members there is a tendency to split into subgroups; and the next 'total' group change does not take place until there are more than twenty-four or twenty-five members. Once there are more than can conveniently hear a member speak without his having to raise his voice to oratorical level or use some mechanical aid, a new dimension will certainly be added.

The smallest number we have so far used for the 'large group' is twenty, the largest fifty. My experience of acting as consultant to a large group is that, with only twenty members, even though they were sitting in two rows, I found it difficult to distinguish sufficiently between behaviour that was due to the largeness of the group and behaviour that I would expect in a smaller study group. Group behaviour was different and more difficult to understand, but I was more aware of the difficulty than of the differences, and, in consequence, felt my interventions to be less effective than they should have been. My experience did, however, lead me to propose that for the next large-group event there should be more than one consultant, if only to avoid my being too selective in what I took up. This account is taken from the experience of Pierre Turquet and myself as joint consultants to large-group events. Even with two of us we found the task difficult, but when we did observe behaviour we were more certain that what we were observing was characteristic of the large group, and was not just extrapolation from small-group experience.

THE ORIGIN OF THE EVENT

My colleagues and I had felt for some time that in our attempts to provide opportunities for members to learn about problems of leadership, we had devised for the most part only small-group situations. The exceptions were the lectures and the opening and closing plenaries. In accordance with the definition of their task and organization the former were 'led' by the lecturers, and the latter by the director and staff. The members had no opportunities to experiment for themselves in large-group situations.

Moreover, for some time we had been unhappy about our conduct of plenary sessions. No matter how well prepared the opening plenary, very little that was said appeared to communicate to members at the manifest level. We were also doubtful, and still are, about appropriate techniques for the plenaries held towards the end of the conference. Indeed, we had had some trouble in defining their primary task – they have been called by various titles: 'evaluations', 'closing plenaries', 'reviews' – and it had even been suggested that they should be dropped entirely. Earlier, we had tried having no formal presentation by a staff member but running the meetings as free-for-all discussions; so far as we could tell, little work had been done in those sessions. We had also tried having various members of the staff give their impressions of what had happened in the conference, as a stimulant to discussion, with little better result.

In the first two conferences after I became director, I reviewed the conference as seen from my role. I gave a lecture which was intended to set a framework for subsequent discussion.[1] Towards the end of the con-

1 For the current position see Chapter 9.

ference that immediately preceded the one in which the large-group event was introduced, I closed my lecture in the following way:

'... work groups can behave with sophistication and maturity, and we can use the basic assumptions to assist task performance; the emotions associated with one basic assumption are then used to control and suppress the emotions associated with others. Mature work groups expect their leaders to mobilize the appropriate assumption for task performance. If the appropriate assumption is dependent, the leader has to be dependable but realistic; if pairing, potent, but with due regard to the limitations of his potency; if fight, constructively aggressive, brave but not foolhardy; if flight, able to extricate the group from a difficult situation, but no coward; nor must he expect to be able to solve all the group's problems in the process of extrication.

This conference ends the day after tomorrow. The task before us and the kind of leadership I have to give seem clear.'

At the time that I gave that review, I had a feeling – shared by most members of the staff – that some of the anger that members felt towards the staff had not come out during the conference, and that we were in danger of finishing without having exposed a major problem of leadership. I had therefore set out to give as good an account as I could of what I thought the conference had been up to. I had tried to give a demonstration of dependable leadership. I hoped that if this could be experienced, then there was a chance that in the remainder of the present session and in the whole of the second session we could mobilize the fight-flight basic assumption, to get into the open some of the anger that had not been expressed, and subsequently mobilize 'flight' as a sophisticated way to end the conference.

I spoke in all for forty-five minutes, making use of many diagrams (based on those prepared for my theoretical lecture on organization (Rice, 1963) to illustrate my theme. I had stated that I was putting forward one framework as a possible basis for the consideration of conference events, and invited others to make alternative suggestions. As soon as I had finished speaking members started to ask questions. At the time I felt strongly that the questions were not asked to clarify what I had said but rather to prolong the lecturer/audience relationship:

'How does this conference compare with others you have held?'

'How do you judge whether a conference has been successful?'

I felt that the members were behaving in this way to avoid the work involved in reviewing the conference experience – though I was less clear than I should have been about what 'review' meant. My evidence was that I was being asked to go on feeding information; but nobody appeared to have taken much notice of the information I had already given. None of the questions seemed to bear any relation to what I had said. I had, of course, to wonder whether what I had said had been so superficial or inaccurate as to be inadequate as a review. I had some evidence that this was not so: while I had been speaking, members had been leaning forward in their chairs, had seemed very attentive, had responded to my mood – laughing at the humour and showing feeling at the more serious passages – and were now paying great deference to me in the way they asked their questions.

With all these feelings inside me I did not answer the questions I had been asked, but I did comment on what I thought the conference was trying to do to me and why. I said I thought that the members were refusing to accept that I had told them what I could, that they still believed that I had all the answers, if only I would, like them, believe in my own omniscience. I explained that if I did this, however, I would fail, and thus give them a justification for ignoring me and what at the moment I symbolized – the conference experience. I pointed out that the questions I had been asked were unrealistic: this conference was not yet finished and so could not be compared with earlier ones; and I wondered how I could measure success, when success was to be judged by what the members had learnt, not by what I had learnt or thought they had.

Members became obviously angry; there were intakes of breath, mutters of 'nonsense', the last questioner looked very aggrieved. Some members subsequently described the incident as 'shocking'. But – and this is where something went wrong – the anger did not really come into the open until after the session. I learned subsequently that groups of members – mainly from study groups – had collected together in the bar and in the common room and had expressed great indignation about the way they had been treated. There was talk of organized protest and much writing of manifestos.

The second session, on the following morning, opened silently. After some desultory discussion one member read out notes that he said resulted from a private members' meeting held on the previous night. He summarized what members had felt about the unfairness of my behaviour, and he acknowledged his own anger, and his frustration at not being able to

73

express it at the time. There was a long silence when he had finished. He then burst out:

'What has happened to all those of you who were expressing so much indignation last night? Why aren't you doing it again now? We have been asked to do it if we want to, but nobody seems to be accepting the invitation.'

Subsequently, members did work at reviewing the conference, but seemed more preoccupied with the problems of review in so large a group than with the conference itself. It was clear that they felt they had had too little experience in working in large groups, at least in the conference setting, to be effective. By not answering questions unless I felt sure that they were genuine inquiries related to the review – a lead followed by other members of the staff who were on the platform – I had destroyed a traditional form of platform/audience organization and had thrown the members back on their own resources.

During that second session members talked to each other, answered each other's questions, argued with each other as well as with the staff, and at one time set up what appeared as a debate with proposer and seconder on one side of the room and opposer and seconder on the other. At that stage I was presumably cast in the role of independent chairman. There was, however, insufficient time or sanction, within the context of a plenary session called to review the conference, to explore all the kinds of organizational machinery that were available and to use them. Some of the anger came out: I had 'blinded them with science', 'put up diagrams of structure to avoid describing the culture', and so on; but there was little time to work out the reasons for these feelings, either real or fantasy.

It is worth noting, in parenthesis, that whatever I did to the members, I certainly mobilized a fight in the staff group, but against myself, and, as with the members, delayed in its manifestation. My colleagues gave me a very rough time in the staff common room after the first plenary session. They expressed considerable dislike of the way I had handled the session, and dismay at the content of my review: it was too complete; did not leave the members anything to say; too facile; too theoretical; they did not know what I had been getting at; could not follow my reasoning and doubted my interpretations of members' behaviour; but they had not felt sure enough of themselves to take me to task in public.

74

THE PRIMARY TASK OF THE LARGE GROUP

The experience of this review and consideration of previous attempts to get work done in plenary reviews suggested that we had set two tasks for plenaries: first, to review the conference, and second, to examine behaviour in a large-group setting. In the review we presumably meant to help members to articulate at least some of their experience, to try to catalogue something of what they had learnt, and to see how they could report when they went back to the organizations that had sent them. We had presupposed some experience of working in large groups but had not provided any opportunities in the conference for such learning other than at lectures and in the intergroup exercise. The task of the intergroup exercise is to examine what is happening in a specific event; it will be discussed in the next chapter. Lectures are traditional, and exchanges between lecturer and audience after the lecture are customary. By delivering a lecture as an opening to the conference review, I had raised legitimate expectations about my subsequent behaviour. By behaving as I did I had affronted the members, and they were right to be angry with me and to complain of 'shock'. Certainly I carried over experience of study groups into the large group and sought to make interpretations of behaviour for which I had no sanction, and which, on reflection, would have been more appropriate to a study group than to a large group.

We have now therefore introduced the large-group event into the conference programme. Its primary task is to study the phenomena of large-group behaviour as they happen. The consultants' role is to help with this task. Their technique is, as in the study group, to use their observations and feelings to enable them to discern what is happening. But now they are faced by more complex phenomena than in the small group. The possible interpersonal relationships and subgroupings are more numerous, anonymity is easier to maintain, and boundaries are more difficult to draw.

THE CONTENT OF THE LARGE GROUP

The same kinds of phenomenon, of course, occur in the large group as in the small face-to-face group. The whole group can act on the same assumption, and often appears to seek to do so, but more frequently the assumption is not unanimous – there is more room for opposition, and more rivals for leadership emerge.

The member of the study group has the problem of relating himself to a few other members. He learns, without structure or directions, to find his way about the various relationships he makes; to say what he feels about others and to accept their feelings about him. When he joins the large group, he has at least two other kinds of relationship available to him: his membership of the study group, with which he has already learnt to identify himself; and his relationships with other members of the conference, some of whom he may know in a different way and more closely outside the conference setting, at home or at work. But other members of the large group, whether previously known to him or not, may themselves be members of other study groups, about whose behaviour and progress he is likely to have become curious. He has probably already discovered at meals and on other social occasions, with some surprise, that, irrespective of different memberships and of different consultants, all study groups are struggling with much the same kinds of problem. In that sense, he can identify with these others as members of the conference going through the same kind of experience. In his own study group, however, he has become identified with his fellow members as individuals; and members of other groups, even though known to him, tend to be seen mainly as outsiders.

In the large group, therefore, in addition to the difficulty of trying to understand his own and others' behaviour, the member of the study group faces many of the others as members of other study groups. He has to face his fantasies about their relationships with each other. He can hardly but project onto them feelings about his own group. He soon finds, however, that when he speaks he speaks as an individual and cannot speak for his group. He has then no group of his own but confronts other groups. He attributes cohesiveness and congruence to other groups that in the large group he cannot feel for his own.

'Why is it that I feel so at home with my study group, but as soon as I come into this room – and (*with a gesture*) there you all are – I no longer feel as though I am at one with you? As soon as I speak, I suddenly feel left on my own.'

'It's bad enough in a small group to feel isolated, but in this room, with this number of people here, and some sitting behind, it's even worse.'

'I'm looking for my friends – those I came here with – but they're in other study groups, they've got different consultants. It's not the same.'

At the opening of one large-group event the furniture available in the room consisted of twelve comfortable armchairs and a large number of hard wooden chairs. For the first session Dr Turquet and I had arranged the comfortable chairs in as small a circle as they would form, with one row, and for parts of the circle two rows, of hard chairs outside them. We occupied two of the comfortable chairs, but sat apart with two chairs between us so that we could not exchange signals or looks without making a movement that would be open for all to see. When the first members came in, they took hard chairs outside the inner circle, some fetching spare chairs that had been pushed out of the way and making a fourth row. Gradually, the inner circle of armchairs filled up, but the members who moved to them did so selfconsciously and defiantly. The last two to arrive took the two comfortable chairs between us. All the time there was a lively chatter going on between members, though all were watching the way the room filled up.

That was the first session; thereafter for the next three sessions a kind of game was played with the seating. When Dr Turquet and I arrived for the second session only two chairs in the inner circle were vacant and they next to each other. I took one of them, but he spontaneously moved to one on the outer ring. At the beginning of the third, all the comfortable chairs were filled when we arrived. Dr Turquet took one in the second row and I one in the third. In discussion some references were made to the seating: the comfort-discomfort, and the need to arrive early to get a comfortable seat; the feeling that the armchairs provided an inner caucus – but the game with the seating was a mild form of test of us. Would we behave differently if we sat in different places? Would we too compete for comfort?

In the first session of one large-group event the lively conversation that had been going on as the members collected died down a few minutes after the official time of starting; there was a brief silence and then a member suggested that they should begin by comparing notes about study groups, a suggestion that was accepted but followed up only in a desultory and general manner; nobody gave any specific details that could be discussed and compared. Members had to keep saying that they were speaking only as individuals and not on behalf of their groups. The problem, it seemed to us – as indeed we commented – was that of establishing the boundaries of the large group. But apparently this could be done only by examining the boundaries that existed within the large group. The study groups, however, existed to study their own behaviour and no member had any sanction to discuss what went on in his study group outside

77

the group. This led to a long discussion about the appropriateness of the large group to study its own behaviour.

'This is not the size of group we would ever use for educational purposes – it is too large. Everybody knows that groups of forty are impossible.'

'The fifty people in this room don't form a group. There's nothing to get hold of.'

Even apart from the difficulty that many members appeared to have with counting, one would have thought from their comments that groups of a similar size never happened outside the conference. The interesting point is perhaps that, at this stage of the large-group event, it does not seem to matter how many actually constitute the group; it is never the appropriate size, and it is always one that does not exist in real life. There is usually little need for the consultants to point out the obvious error – in the large group some member will not only draw attention to it, but will also give an explanation for the denial:

'I seem to be the only person in this room who regularly has to deal with groups of this size! I don't believe it and I think we're all avoiding our job here now.'

At this point it is not unusual for some member to confess that, although he cannot rely on the support of his study group for anything he says, he has spent the first few minutes looking round to make sure that all his fellow members are present:

'Well, my study group is all here, I've counted, and somehow, this is comforting.'

But others, quick to note any sense of complacency, ask if that is because he thinks his group is better than any other, and the discussion about study-group and large-group boundaries tends to be resumed. The same discussion occurs at intervals during the event, and, at times, one cannot avoid the impression that, by contrast with the large group, the study group appears as a warm, cosy, intimate group with a well-defined task and a serious sense of purpose – an impression that is quite contrary to the reality of any study group of which I have been a member or to which I have been a consultant. In the later sessions it is possible to draw attention to the small groups as the keepers of the large-group morality; to demonstrate that, though in the large group they may appear to dissolve, yet, symbolically, they are points of reference that determine the way in which individuals should be treated, even if in the large group they are treated quite differently.

By the second or third session, periods of which have been frankly dull and boring, the attempts to use study groups or other groupings that arise outside the large group as alternatives to the large group are acknowledged to have yielded little result, and attention is turned to the large group itself. Attempts to define the boundaries in terms of the task invariably fail. There are always too many members ready to say that they feel nothing; that they have no sense of loyalty to the group as a group; and when challenged about why they are there, they talk either of hoping to learn something, or of doubting that they will come again or even stay for the particular session:

'I don't feel anything here, nothing happens. Nobody has any constructive suggestions to make. But we could all do one thing – we could leave, and not meet tomorrow.'

In one group, this question gave rise to an alternative proposal, which was to split into smaller groups to discuss the problem and then report back to the whole:

'If we split here (*making a gesture that separated Dr Turquet and myself*), we might have more chance of coming to some conclusion.'

This suggestion led to a lively discussion, in which two parties were formed – the split and the anti-split. The discussion became acrimonious, the anti-split party arguing that to split would defeat the object of the exercise; the split party demanding some kind of 'experiment', even if the experiment jeopardized the continuation of the large group. During these exchanges – which went on intermittently for several sessions – Dr Turquet and I tried to clarify what we thought to be happening. We pointed to the apparent need to find some abstract concept outside the group to which we could subscribe; to the need to have something – an ideal, a faith, or an enemy – which would define the group's boundaries and allow a leader to arise to embody the group purpose. A rational task was not enough. The alternative appeared to be to find the in- and out-groups within the large group itself – each with its own recognized leaders. We made the hypothesis that what was feared was the undirected, unstructured power of the group, the fear of its potential violence. We took as our evidence the comfort and liveliness of the acrimonious debate that had developed, the reassurance that was felt as soon as an anti-group had been

79

found to oppose the power of the group, the attempt to split us by enlisting us into opposing camps. If the group could neither find something outside itself to give it definition, nor guarantee acceptable and conflicting parties within, the only possibility appeared to be complete impotence, or discussion that dealt only in trivialities:

'It seems we can be united only if we are split; we can become one only if we are more than one.'

This theme, with more sophisticated variations, and with discussions of its parallels in real life – party politics and the concept of parliament, management and trade unions – is a constant preoccupation of the large group. How to control the potential destructiveness of the large group, and the fear that, in spite of individual choice, it could get out of hand in a crisis. At times one of us has been awarded a halo and the other horns; there have been attempts – part realistic and part fanciful – to analyse the differences between us as role-takers and, far less directly, as persons. Escape into laughter is easy, but the impression is of passing time rather than of working.

Time and time-keeping become important. It is as though time itself can provide a boundary; that the large group exists only for the time of the session and what happens in between starting and stopping the session is irrelevant. But the testing of this boundary soon proves that it is fragile. In one session of a large-group event nearly all the members were sitting in the room some five or more minutes early. Everyone appeared to be in lively conversation with his nearby neighbours. At the time the session was due to start there was a sudden silence – and nobody apparently had anything to say. After some minutes a fitful discussion started about the difficulty of talking in the large group, and when the contrast between immediately before and immediately after the starting time was pointed out, some members said that the earlier talking had been between individuals and that there had been no group 'present'. At the following session, though members were obviously aware of the time, as shown by the numerous glances at watches, there was no sharp dividing line, and the boundary of time had been broken.

At other sessions there have been suggestions to leave early, or to move out and move in again; and members have tried experiments, sometimes singly, sometimes in small groups. But none of the experiments has aroused much feeling in the group as a whole. Those who have left one session early have been accepted at the following session without question or with only casual non-caring questions about how they felt. Those who have announced that they were going out

> 'for ten minutes, and will then return to test whether what one of the consultants said yesterday about our being afraid to go out because we might not be allowed in again is true or not,'

have themselves, on their return, not been sure whether they have proved anything.

But leaving that is due not to deliberate experiment but to group and personal pressures has given ample evidence of the fear of the potential indiscriminate destructiveness of the large unstructured group. At one conference, the fourth session of a seven-session large-group event coincided with a first division football match in the city. About six members chose the football match instead of the session. They just did not turn up. On the same day another member had to be away at a function in his own job and he had announced this in advance. In spite of his friends' protestations that he had apologized in advance and even that a condition of his being released to attend the conference had been his fulfilling this particular engagement, there was far more discussion of his absence and of his motives for it than of the absence and motives of those who had gone to the football match.

Later in the session the group referred to the empty chairs that had been left in the second row by the absentees and asked the three who were in the third row – of whom I was one – to move. After some discussion about my sitting where I was, and an invitation to move, which I did not accept, the group turned to the two others. One announced that he liked it where he was and was staying there; the other commented that he felt more a part of the group than he had ever felt before:

> '. . . probably because I feel that it is the first time that anybody has paid any attention to me. It appears you have to get outside this group to get anybody in it to take any notice of you.'

There was some discussion of leading from outside and of nihilism inside, and the member then got up, saying:

'Since you want to complete the circle I will now join you,'

but as he moved to an empty chair in the second row:

'How do you know we want you now?'

and he was left, embarrassed, being invited by some to sit down and being asked by others if he felt welcome. He sat down, but within seconds he got up saying:

'It seems I'm not wanted, so I'll go,'

and left the room. As he went, the discussion returned immediately to those who were sitting outside the circle: why they did it and what effect it had on the group. After some minutes one member burst out:

'I believe we have just committed an act of violence,'

to be followed by an outbreak of statements about why the particular member had just left. He had not wanted to come; he had said at the beginning that if the session was as futile as the last one, he would leave before the end; it had always been his intention to go – statements that were belied by his obvious embarrassment and discomfort, and his hesitation both on his way to the door and when he got there. Both Dr Turquet and I drew attention to the way we were all shedding responsibility for what had happened, blaming it all on the individual. This led to a long and acrimonious discussion about who had said what and why, and there were moves to stop the session at once. Those who, up to this time, had been silent then started to express their concern, their feeling of helplessness:

'I can't understand how we could be so heartless, I'm shocked by our cruelty to — and we still sit here doing nothing. I feel terrible about it and I'm doing nothing. I can't avoid the responsibility, but I can't carry it either.'

In subsequent sessions when this member had returned, and so had those who had been to the football match, it was acknowledged that the person they had wanted to get at was me, but they had picked somebody else sitting 'outside' the group instead; and that even getting at me was a displacement of their anger at those who had attended the football match, and thus expressed their contempt for the group and its activities. My own responsibility as director in having so arranged the programme that the session coincided with the football match was not taken up until two sessions later, and by that time the mood of the group was one in which the conference in general and the large group in particular were being idealized as a learning situation, and there were too many ready to leap to my defence for the hostility to be very manifest.

The need for some form of structure, however rudimentary, is often shown by the ease with which the attention of the group can be focused. At the beginning of a session, closing the door, somebody moving his chair, even coughing, seems enough to bring the meeting to order. Subsequently, just standing up to make a statement stops all discussion at once, or, if anybody does go on talking, he or she is told in no uncertain terms to shut up. But such rudimentary structures are accepted for the relief they bring – somebody is going to do something, anything, so long as it avoids examination of what lies behind behaviour here and now. Any attempt to look seriously at an incident such as that described above can lead to anarchy, in which any constructive suggestion is either destroyed at once or, equally effective from the point of view of avoiding real work at studying behaviour, blown up to preposterous proportions. On one occasion the suggestion that we should look at what had just happened had become, before the end of the session, a proposal to appoint a secretary to write the history of the large group and of the other events of the conference that impinged on the large group. The session ended with a spurious voting procedure which, like so many voting procedures, was quite inconclusive, and by which nobody felt, or perhaps even had the slightest intention of feeling, bound.

As the group grows more experienced in dealing with an unfamiliar situation there is some recognition that the group and those who lead it can be used by individual members for the projection of many of their more primitive impulses. Unlike the small group, for which as a member the individual accepts some responsibility, the large group, being so difficult to control, so anonymous, can be an easier receptacle of feelings and urges that most of us would disown.

'Yes, this ties up with what I learnt last night. When I accused people of being childish and then I had a discussion with one of the people I had so accused, I recognized that what made me so angry was the childish part of myself which I had put into them.'

'I divide people into three kinds: there are those I think agree with me; there are those who don't but I think I can work with them and discuss it; and there are those I don't even want to talk to, and they are the bastards in here.'

'Now I've been sitting here all this time and nobody has done anything to me. I've wanted to know how people have been feeling, but I haven't dared to ask – but I've learnt I can't absolve myself from responsibility for what this group, of which I am a member, has been doing to other

83

people, even though I've been sitting back doing nothing. People all round the room have at various times in these sessions shown that they need help, but all we do is just sit back.'

'The painful thing I have learnt about myself is my willingness to sacrifice others.'

This use of the large group also means that if an individual feels he has something good to contribute – and members made many insightful comments – then the very contribution arouses all his own paranoid fantasies. He fears in advance that it will be destroyed and that the group will do it. But because it is also a part of himself that will contribute to the destruction he hesitates, and does not express his real feelings until he has found out if he is going to get support.

'Why didn't you put it more clearly and make it a proper proposition?'

'Well, I wanted an echo before I could do anything definite. I was just talking, waiting, but if there's an echo and I have support, yes, I will propose . . . .'

'I see bits of myself in everybody here, and some of them I don't like.'

The recognition that many of the organizations we invent, the controls we accept in our everyday life, are not so much constructive attempts to solve our problems as defences against our own lightly buried primitive impulses can be painful. So also can be the recognition that what we find so difficult to tolerate, and will go to considerable lengths to deny, is uncertainty about our decisions and inability to understand our own human problems.

CONSULTANTS TO THE LARGE GROUP

I do not know how many consultants there should be to how large a group. I have so far worked on my own and with one other colleague. On my own I found myself bewildered by much that was happening; I would no sooner work out something to my own satisfaction than I would realize that a change had taken place. I was always trying to catch up with my own thinking and feeling. I found myself at the end of sessions unable to recall what had happened or what had been said, and quite empty of ideas. When I have worked with Pierre Turquet I have felt reassured by his presence. I might not know what is happening, but he might. And if he has not known either, then at least a colleague whose insight I respect and trust is in equal difficulty and I can comfort myself that it may not be entirely my own stupidity or insensitivity that is leading me astray.

More positively, I believe we have complemented each other in the events we have taken together, seeing sometimes the same evidence but from different points of view, and sometimes different pieces of evidence that have been mutually illuminating. We have each had, in the other, a point of reference, and in analysing our feelings for each other we have, I am sure, been able to see more clearly what the group has been doing to us. In our discussions after the sessions we have at least both been talking about the same events and have been able to compare our reactions to them and to each other's interventions. In particular, in both sessions and subsequent discussions we have been able to study the roles in which we have been cast by the group and which we have accepted or rejected, and our reasons for acceptance and rejection. And when we have both been bewildered, we have, in some measure, been able to ask each other why; and when, as has sometimes happened, we have found different reasons for our bewilderment, the very differences have enabled us to understand what the group was projecting onto us to cause it.

I think that so far we have both found it more difficult to maintain austere professional roles in large groups than in study groups. By that I mean that we have both entered more into the mood of the group, laughing at the jokes, worrying about individuals, feeling helpless to stop somebody's being hurt and guilty about our own inaction. But that, maybe, is because neither of us is yet sufficiently skilful.

The phenomena with which we deal in the large group are more primitive, more complex, and more diffuse than in the small group; intervention has to be more direct and forceful. The most important characteristic of the large group is that it is large. Without an abstract ideal or an external enemy its boundaries are difficult to define; without boundaries, and hence without even an elemental structure, action is impulsive and hence potentially dangerous; the group's very freedom to experiment can become anarchy. The study of the large group as a group is thus made the more difficult because the object of study is itself so tenuous. In this emotional climate the members turn to the consultants for reassurance that they, at least, can control the violence; the fear, and it is shared by the consultants, is that they too will be unable to act quickly or wisely enough to avert disaster.

Again because of its size, and the amount of 'noise' – in engineering terms – it can create, the large group is able to ignore its task and its consultants for a long time. Denial of difficulty, refusal to look at what is happening, are easier. Distractions are many, and as consultants we frequently found ourselves distracted, but without being aware of it, without being so certain, as in a study group, that what we were observing was intended to distract. We both found ourselves fed with so much information that we frequently floundered in out attempts to extract what was relevant to the task of the group, to distinguish when it was working at its task and when it was playing. As individuals, we have to be aware of, and accept, a close scrutiny of our behaviour, as distinct from what we say. Members concentrate less on us as individuals than on the similarities and differences between us, denying the differences when they want us to be united to hold the group together, emphasizing them when they want to split the group and to play one of us off against the other. We have to use our own awareness of our support for each other and of our conflicts to test the reality of their feelings against their projections upon us.

Sometimes we answer questions directly, but attempt so far as we can to answer them in the light of the task we have set ourselves. As on one occasion, when Pierre Turquet was asked if he would express his real feelings now, he replied:

'Bewildered.'

And that faced the group with the problem of his fallibility, at a time when they had been trying to believe him omniscient. In the large group, even more than in the small group, the consultant is very tempted to take a traditional leadership role; the need for a leader and for structure is so manifest and the fear of violence is so great. It is easier in the large group to forget that groups can also be constructive, and so allow oneself to be seduced into trying to be its saviour.

THE LARGE GROUP IN THE CONFERENCE

Members of earlier conferences in which there was no large-group event, who have attended recent ones for more advanced training,[1] have told us that the large group appears to be dealing with what, at previous conferences, had to be dealt with by the members in their own informal meetings. At first there appeared to be some danger that the large group

1 See Chapter 13.

would become a mopping-up operation, and would thus put all small groups together – study groups, intergroup exercise, and application groups – and avoid the contrasts of experience that these different events were intended to afford. We now believe that it is an experience in its own right, and that it adds a new dimension to the learning situations provided, offering an opportunity that some members of previous conferences used to make for themselves. When that happened, however, the results could not then manifest themselves until the plenary review sessions, and then, because the end of the conference was so near, they could not be adequately worked out in the remaining time.

The large group is the one event, apart from the more formal plenaries, in which members can experience the forces that a large group brings to bear on its leaders, in a setting where the prescribed task is to study those forces. Because the large group does contain the total membership, it is the first event to end, and thus offers an appropriate preparation for ending. It provides the first experience of the need for mourning.

It is the event in which the individual finds again that he has to take personal responsibility for his actions. If he is to behave in a mature and adult manner, he cannot just dissolve into the group, but has to accept the responsibility for stopping something of which he disapproves, or the guilt for not doing so. But to get to this realization he has to be prepared to examine many of the myths and value systems he has previously accepted with few questions: that the 'goodness' or 'badness' of groups depends entirely on the 'goodness' or 'badness' of the individuals who make them up; that on matters of principle majorities and minorities have very much relevance; that structure and leadership are always positive and not, as they are found to be, defences against anxiety. He has to be prepared to question many of the beliefs and attitudes that in a complex modern society support most of its social, political, and working institutions. He has to face the difficulty of tolerating uncertainty about outcomes and the inability always to understand human affairs. He also has to learn to recognize that, in the chaotic complexity in which so much of human life is lived, simple solutions provided by dogmatic leaders work only if the reality of the complexity is denied.

CHAPTER 7

The Intergroup Exercise

In the first intergroup exercise in the 1959 conference, the members were asked to split into groups in any way they wished and, by negotiations between the groups, to decide on the content of four sessions in the conference programme. They were provided with a summary of information gathered from registration forms that they had filled in before coming to the conference. These forms included a section on 'special interests' not covered by the formal conference programme. Members were also given information about the staff's competence to deal with some of the topics listed. The members succeeded in filling the sessions allocated to them, albeit with some difficulty. The staff tasks were seen as responding to requests for expert help with particular topics and, at the same time, helping members to learn about intergroup processes.

In subsequent conferences the same task, that of filling sessions, was given to the members, but the task of the staff was seen as concentrating on the relations between the groups that were formed for this purpose. At the 1959 conference, members were invited to choose their own method of dividing into groups; in later conferences they were allocated by the staff, as for study and application groups.

Among the staff there has always been discussion about the different tasks of the intergroup exercise and about the desirability of defining one of them as the 'primary task'. Was it to fill spare sessions of the conference, to deal with members' interests that were not otherwise catered for, or to learn about intergroup relations? The staff group itself did not seem clear, and there was evidence that the confusion extended to the members. Preparation for the sessions that were filled as a result of the exercise always involved members in considerable spare-time activity, and the sessions themselves did not appear to give much satisfaction to either members or staff. When the exercise, as an exercise, was reviewed before the planned sessions had taken place, the review was affected by doubts about the plans and, when the plans had been implemented, there was dissatisfaction with performance. More particularly, in the review members often commented that consultants to member groups interfered with the task of filling sessions by drawing attention to what was going on in the 'here and now'. I have always found it difficult to accept that an 'interpretation' of behaviour that hinders rather than helps task performance can ever be justified. But where there are two or even three tasks, help with one of them can clearly interfere with performance of the others. I recognize, of course, that the comments of members might not be anything more than projections of their own sense of futility at the results of their efforts and that the consultants might be acting as scapegoats for members' own dissatisfaction with what they have accomplished. Equally, I have always felt that while confusion between the different tasks existed, so would the role of consultants be confused and hence their ability to help diminished. Members' opportunities for learning about intergroup processes would therefore also be limited.

THE PRIMARY TASK OF THE INTERGROUP EXERCISE

The more precise formulation of the task of the total conference helped us to simplify that of the intergroup exercise. Special interests that fell outside the total conference task became irrelevant and were therefore dropped. Members are now asked, before they come to a conference, in what way the conference task has particular relevance for their work. This simplification, however, still left two tasks to the intergroup exercise. If we were to define a primary task, we had two possibilities. The first would be to drop the task of learning about intergroup relations to minor status. The primary task of the exercise would be to fill a number of sessions. Staff might be able to help with this task, and in so doing might make comments about intragroup and intergroup processes, but such comments would be appropriate only if they helped with the primary task. To direct attention to the study of intragroup or intergroup relations for their own sake would be inappropriate. For the most part, staff would try to observe how the intrusion of problems of intergroup relations helped or hindered task performance. If they believed them to be helping, they would do nothing; if hindering, try to remove the hindrance. In the review session, staff would then have to take a teaching role and disclose the results of their observations.

This is a valid way of learning about intergroup processes but it has to be recognized that it is a by-product of primary task performance.

The second possibility was to define the primary task as the study of intergroup relationships. The filling of sessions or any other subsidiary task would then become a vehicle for this purpose. Experience of earlier conferences suggested that the study of intergroup relations was difficult, and the danger of providing a vehicle other than the subject of study was that the vehicle became more important than the journey. It therefore seemed to those of us who are now running the conferences about which I write that we should attempt one task only and that it should be the study of intergroup relations. In the choice of method we had no doubt that, in order to be consistent with the purpose of the conference as a whole, we should try to provide experience rather than theory, and this meant that we should study intergroup relations as they happen.

Various experiments have been tried since that decision was taken. I should emphasize that the account given here is my version of the intergroup exercise and of its place in a residential conference. Many of my colleagues feel that I have sometimes used my authority as conference director to impose my design on the exercise and that I confuse directorship of the exercise with that of the conference. I do not at present believe that in a residential conference these two roles can be adequately differentiated by the members (let alone myself), and I think that it is better to accept the confusion and try to learn from it than attempt to set up artificial structures to avoid it. This problem is discussed in a later section of this chapter, and in Chapter 11. What follows is therefore an account of where my thinking about intergroup exercises in residential conferences has reached. For illustration I shall, however, use some incidents from exercises held on non-residential courses. My colleagues are already experimenting with different methods in non-residential settings, and will give their own accounts of them. In the course of time it should be possible to carry out controlled experiments to enable us to assess what is learnt from the various approaches.

For a group to communicate as a group, it has to have a 'voice'. For the 'voice' to be coherent and understandable, not only outside the group, but inside as well, some mechanism, some 'political' machinery has to be devised. This enables a group to agree on what its 'voice' is to say. It also has to agree on a mechanism for the reception of communications from other groups, and on a framework of beliefs and attitudes within which it can interpret these communications.

Representation involves at least four kinds of relationship:

1. Between a representative and the group he represents or is supposed to represent: the group has to come to terms with what it believes is being, or has been, said on its behalf; and the representative has to come to terms with the often confused policy and messages he has to communicate.

2. Between a representative of one group and the group he is visiting on behalf of his own group: he has to be sure of the role he is taking, and of the role he is being put into by the group he is visiting. The group has to interpret his message and his role and come to terms with discrepancies between them.

3. Between representatives from different groups: this is affected by the extent to which each representative is believed to be loyal to his own group, by the credibility of the point of view he expresses, and by the growth of in-group feeling among representatives – the extent to which the representatives form a group of their own in conflict with the groups they represent.

4. Among those who are represented but left behind when the representative has gone to represent them. The remaining members of the group have to deal with doubts and fears about how they are being represented, and with the effect this has on them and on their attitude to what they have done or not done.

There are also, of course, the relationships between members of various groups when they hear, through other channels of communication outside the exercise, what impressions their representatives are making on other groups, and what other groups are thereby inferring about themselves:

This list could be continued. Each relationship can affect all the others, and difficulty in any one area can destroy the constructive intentions that groups may have about their relations with other groups. Most of the problems of negotiation, and their concomitant difficulties about leadership, loyalty, and confidentiality, are involved.

Broadly speaking, three kinds of representation can be differentiated. It matters less what titles are used to distinguish the different types of representative than that the differences in their functions should be clearly understood:

(a) Observer: a representative dispatched to find out what is happening elsewhere, to try to obtain information from other groups, but without any sanction to express views or to take action on behalf of his own group. His job is to observe, but not to give information.

(b) Delegate: a representative sent out to deliver a message, express a given point of view, or take a given action on behalf of his group. He represents, but has no sanction to vary the message, the view he is expressing, or the action he is taking in the light of what he finds outside. If a delegate finds that he cannot get an answer to his message, that the point of view he is expressing is not acceptable, that the action proposed is not feasible, he has to refer back to his group before making any changes on its behalf.

(c) Plenipotentiary: a representative sent out with flexible terms of reference. He is to do the best he can in the light of the known views or known policies of his own group. He may be given limits beyond which he cannot go but within these terms of reference he can commit his group to a view or to a course of action.

Clearly, there are many variations in the precise power that a representative may exercise, and he may combine the functions of more than one kind of representative, depending on the constraints put upon him in the light of a prediction of the circumstances he is going to meet. The definitions of observer, delegate, and plenipotentiary are three points on a continuum. There can be more than one observer, delegate, or plenipotentiary; communications and negotiations between groups can be public or private; groups can send out a mixed team of plenipotentiaries, observers, delegates, and other variations. The problems for the group and its representative lie in the precision with which responsibility and authority can be defined and in the certainty with which the group can predict the behaviour of other groups in the environment in relation to itself.

THE STRUCTURE OF THE INTERGROUP EXERCISE

I have said earlier that when members first arrive at the conference the event that appears to cause them most anxiety is the study group, and for this reason the study group is put into the conference at an early stage. Once the study groups have become established, the large-group exercise is introduced to give members a chance of experiencing the different problems that arise and the difficulties of leading and following in such a setting.

In particular, they learn how they feel when all the study groups are brought together. The study of intergroup relations is put in after the large group has met at least twice. The sequence of the events is geared to the increasing complexity in the variables involved in leadership. Starting with a small face-to-face group, members move into the large group and then to the intergroup event. I believe that the intergroup exercise would perhaps be more effective if the large group could meet more often before the exercise starts, but the time available for conferences places constraints on programme flexibility.

I have also discussed in earlier chapters the many possible identifications and differences among the members. They are drawn from different backgrounds; but some are more closely identified with each other outside the conference than within it; many have professional links through the kind of work they are doing, and may or may not be members of the same organization; others know each other socially. Within the conference itself they are already members of study groups, and are to become members of application groups. The staff also come from different institutions or different parts of the same institution, and have usually been trained in different disciplines. In a recent conference the staff came from the Universities of Leicester and Bristol, the Prison Department of the Home Office, the Tavistock Institute, and the Tavistock Clinic. Members of the staff also appear in different roles in the various events in the conference.

In general, then, possible intergroup relations within the conference are numerous and complex. However, within the setting of the conference itself, and in particular at the beginning of the intergroup exercise, the dominant intergroup relationship present in the room as the exercise starts is that between the staff, who are running the exercise, and the members, who are to take part in it.

At this stage there are four major differences between members and staff:

1. There are more members than staff. The members form a large group; the staff, a small face-to-face working group.

2. The job of the staff is to help members to learn about intergroup relations, not to study them for their own sake. That is not to say that the staff do not also learn by taking part in the event. Indeed, one of the difficulties of writing this account is that I feel I learn so much in each exercise that what I write will be out of date before it can be published. But staff learning is secondary to their main job. Members, on

the other hand, may or may not take the opportunities provided; they have no particular obligation, beyond being present, to take part in the event at all.

3. The staff know more about the running of an intergroup exercise than do the members. Though it did not feel as if this was so the first time that such an exercise was held, the justification for staff membership is that they know enough to help members to learn. Whether by the end of an exercise the members would accept this particular difference, the staff at least have been through it before, and have some idea of the kind of experience to expect.

4. Perhaps most important, the staff already have a 'political' organization. By contrast, the members have not as a rule achieved, or needed to achieve, any kind of organization among themselves. They have no mechanism by which they can communicate as a body of members to the staff, even if they have anything to communicate. I hold office by virtue of the authority vested in me by the other members of the staff. I am, in that sense, 'elected', but in terms of the total conference the franchise is small and powerful. How good the organization of the staff is may, of course, be one of the objects of study in the intergroup exercise. How far I can 'direct' the exercise may be called into question. How far what the staff have delegated to me and what I, in turn, have delegated to them, represent what the original delegation meant, and how far as the 'representative' of the staff I represent the staff point of view may also be tested.

THE RULES OF THE EXERCISE

Because there are more members than can form a face-to-face group, a number of rooms are made available for members' meetings. The number is limited, but is sufficient to allow members to split into face-to-face groups. They may split into more and smaller groups if they wish, but, so far as the staff are concerned, the territorial boundaries of members' groups are fixed by the rooms allocated for this purpose. A space is also designated for the staff group. Whenever the building allows it, this space is in a hall or on a landing. The idea behind this location is that as a part of the provision of learning opportunities the staff relationships will be conducted in public. The lecture room in which plenary sessions take place is designated as common to all groups for intergroup meetings.

In addition to these arrangements concerning space for meetings, a number of staff members are made available to help member groups in their study of the problems of intergroup relations. If the members split into more groups than the number of staff available, then there are no staff to help some of them. If they split into a smaller number of groups than there are staff available, or if they do not call on staff help, then some staff are left unemployed as group consultants. Members are given the right to call or not to call on help from staff members. Another member of staff is designated as consultant to the staff group and to meetings between representatives or between whole groups. In the definitions of representatives used earlier, the staff who are called on for help are pleni-potentiaries: the policy within which they operate is laid down in advance – to help members to learn about intergroup relations; within that policy, they do the best they can in the circumstances in which they find themselves.

We have frequently discussed the problem of whether the staff should be assigned to rooms and go there irrespective of whether the members use those rooms. So far, at any rate, I have always held the view that to assign staff members to rooms, whether groups of members meet in them or not, is begging the question of whether members can learn more or less by being given the right to accept or to reject help. If staff consultants are allocated to rooms, members going into a room within the bounds of the exercise automatically get the services of the staff member there, and the problem of not getting help is complicated for them by their having to find another room and put themselves outside the territorial boundaries of the exercise in order to avoid it.

We have also considered whether groups of members should have the right to ask for specific staff members, and hence raise for members the problem of competition for different staff members, and for staff the problem of why some are preferred to others. This particular variation, with the problems it will give rise to, should, I think be tried. So far however, in order to simplify the exercise for members and staff we have named the staff who are to act as consultants to groups of members, and have laid down the order in which they will be made available (usually alphabetically on the first demand and thereafter in rotation).

Members of staff who are not available as consultants to groups or to intergroup meetings, or who, if available, are not called on, form the staff group, and as such represent the management of the exercise. Consultants in groups are there to help members but they are also repre-sentatives of the staff group. Hence anything that is said or done in their presence can be communicated to the staff group. But it is emphasized that the staff will not act as representatives of member groups; that is, they will not communicate from member group to member group via the staff group.

The last session of the exercise, whatever state has been reached, consists of a review held in plenary session.

By the rules the only identifiable group that remains constant throughout the exercise is the staff group. The members may split or not as they wish, they may have staff help or not as they wish; they may or may not set up a system for intergroup communication. The only disciplines imposed are on the staff members: the roles they will take, and the territory and time within which they will take cognizance of what is happening. No rules are laid down for member' behaviour or even for their participation. Just as members will discuss what is happening in the exercise outside the event, so, of course, will the staff discuss it among themselves as well, but in the exercise they are concerned only with what is happening in front of them and then only in so far as it relates to intergroup relations.

THE BEGINNING OF THE EXERCISE

So far all the intergroup exercises have been opened in plenary session, by the director's stating briefly the concepts behind its design and announcing the rules that have been described above.[1] When I have done this I have been accompanied on the platform by the staff members taking part, seated in groups according to their roles in the exercise. At the end of my statement I have passed the exercise over to the members. Before we had differentiated between the roles of 'director' and 'consultant to intergroup meetings', the whole staff stayed in the room at this stage. In recent exercises I have finished my statement by asking if there are any questions and, when these have been dealt with, I have then led the staff from the room to the staff 'territory'.

At the conference where this type of exercise was first tried, and the staff stayed when I had finished my statement, the room was emptied within twenty-five seconds. On that occasion I had stood to make my

---

[1] On one occasion, before we had invented the role of 'consultant to the staff group and to intergroup meetings', Pierre Turquet acted as director of the exercise and I as consultant to a group.

statement. As I sat down, and indeed before I had resumed my seat, members were on the move out of the room. As they went, they called on the various staff members who had been named as consultants to go with them. At the time it was tempting to think of an organized plot, but such evidence as was available suggested that this could not be so. Members looked far too puzzled about what they were doing. Odd remarks were picked up as they went, such as:

'What does he expect *us* to do now?'

'Well, I'm going to find a group that at least has some women in it this time!' (*This was from a member of a study group composed entirely of men.*)

It may be that some members had a conscious plan, though nobody ever admitted to it, and put this plan into effect. The move having started, others followed. It seemed quite clear, however, that though there may not have been any conscious plan, there was an unconscious agreement, and that, at the simplest level, was to get out of the room as quickly as possible. Members were running away from somebody or something. But the question that had to be answered was from whom or from what? They were not running away from the staff as staff, since those who had been designated as consultants to member groups were asked to go with them; nor, at the time, did they appear to be avoiding the problem of splitting into groups, since they took that problem with them, as was evidenced by the amount of tramping about and banging of doors in the various rooms allocated for members' meetings. The only conclusion I could come to was that they wanted to get away from me. I could not believe from what had been happening in the rest of the conference that I was so hated that members could not bear to be in the same room with me. I could only conclude that for some reason they did not want to tackle the task of building their own 'political' machinery in front of me. I now believe that I only symbolized the problem, and, as I shall show, the same phenomenon has occurred even when all the staff have left the room. Experience of the large group suggests that the flight is from the fear of the potential violence of unstructured groups. It is not rational but impulsive. I still think that the interpretation that the flight was from me in my role of director was not entirely incorrect, but that I greatly exaggerated the importance of the authority symbol I represented. The only way I could have stopped the flight was by exercising authority structurally, that is by telling the members how to split or, at least, by asking them to discuss a particular way of splitting.

The second time an exercise of this kind was held (on a non-residential course in London), some members who had taken part in the residential exercise were members of the course and therefore present. They knew what had happened on the residential course. In addition, many other members of the course had heard stories about the exercise. Nevertheless, no sooner had I finished the opening statement than some members started to move out of the room. Those who had previous experience of the problems that such flight could cause immediately tried to stop the stampede. They said that members should stay in the room to decide how they could most profitably split up to learn about intergroup relations. These voices, however, had no effect and all the members had left, including those who had tried to stop the move, within a minute and a half.

On the third occasion I was not director of the exercise, and Dr Turquet took this role. He introduced some variations into the procedure, one of which was to send the consultant staff off to the rooms that they were going to occupy before he finished his statement. Even so, the room cleared in just over one minute after he had finished. On the fourth occasion, after asking if there were any questions and receiving none, I led the staff from the room. The last staff to leave were almost pushed out of the way by the members following them. Had we not had our previous experience, I do not see how we could have avoided the interpretation that I had led the flight myself.

Only once so far, on a non-residential course in London, have we repeated the exercise with the same members. The first exercise had, like others, concluded with a review in the course of which the reasons for the rapid emptying of the room had been discussed. On the whole, the interpretation, similar to the one given above, had been accepted. At the repeat, members said that they were determined to discuss the problem of splitting, not just to split as they had done the first time. But most of the discussion turned into members asking questions of the staff – about the previous review, about the rules of the exercise, about what I had said and done:

'It's two months since we did it, we've forgotten the rules you laid down.'

'Well, we've not exactly forgotten them, but we've distorted them.'

'Why don't you just repeat them?'

98

When I replied that I was sure that everybody knew perfectly well what the rules were since they were so simple and so few, and that I believed I was being asked to repeat them as a means of avoiding or at least postponing examination of member-staff relations in general and of my leadership in particular, there followed a long discussion that started from the difficulty of considering staff-member relationships. However, this soon turned again into a discussion of the previous exercise and members admitted that once the stampede had happened they had all been flabbergasted by it. After some time, there seemed to be a consensus of opinion that because of the flight from the problem of splitting into groups the last intergroup exercise had been a complete disaster. But nobody wanted to query in what sense the word 'disaster' was being used. If, as everyone agreed, the members' failure to set up any political machinery was a 'disaster', then the assumption must have been that the primary task of the exercise was to learn how to set up political machinery. Yet almost any member of that course, given the task of devising and creating joint consultative machinery or a committee to discuss ways and means, could have done so in a very short time. The important question that could not be answered was whether they had learnt anything about the relations between themselves as members of groups involved in intergroup relations. The solid attendance at the second exercise implied that, if the last had been a disaster, they were prepared to face another.

Eventually, an hour after the opening, a number of members said that they were getting nowhere and would get nowhere while they stayed as a total group. Five people got up and started to move out of the room; three others followed them immediately. The rest then split themselves into two groups by some process of selection that was not disclosed and moved into the other two rooms available for the exercise.

THE CONTENT OF A GROUP MEETING

Immediately after the split, groups express concern about themselves as groups; why the particular members who have assembled in any one room have been there is hardly questioned. So far, in most of the conferences that have been held, an examination of group composition after the split has shown that the exercise groups consist either of the existing study groups, when the number of rooms available has equalled the

99

number of study groups – a situation we try to avoid if we can – or of an equal number of members from each study group. The possibility that these compositions could have happened so often by chance is so small as to make it virtually certain that study-group membership has for the time being overwhelmed any other kind of group membership inside, or outside, the conference. So far as members have been concerned with intergroup relations, they have been more concerned at first with those between study groups than those between themselves as members and the staff. In effect, they have chosen the easier boundaries to work with.

When the split has been into study groups, members have sought to continue study-group experience, but in a setting in which what is happening 'outside' becomes a legitimate subject for study; that is, a study group in which the group cannot be accused of 'flight' when it discusses something 'out there' instead of 'in here'. In another sense members have also expressed hostility to management for being asked to perform some other task and have proposed to continue an experience that has become familiar.

When members have split into groups that comprise an equal number from each study group, they have usually tried to conduct the intergroup exercise within the groups so formed. They have started to discuss the similarities and differences between study groups. It is as though they do what they have been told to do – namely, study intergroup relations – but in such a way that they can avoid having to come to terms with problems either of representation or of their relations with authority. This involves denying that the staff consultants are members of a staff group and that the relations established with a consultant are relations with another group. It is also, of course, an attempt to split the staff acting as consultants from the staff group, and hence from conference management. If consultants can be beguiled into acting as study-group leaders, then they can be set up as leaders in breaking the rules laid down for the exercise, and hence management authority can be destroyed.

The initial preoccupation of most groups, in other words, is their own identity. At first, they avoid the nature of the split, the panic that they feel, thus:

'I went out of the room, and just looked over the banisters to see who was following me.'

'We two walked away together and found four others going into the same room. That started it.'

'I couldn't understand what was happening. I was flabbergasted, everybody else seemed to be going somewhere, so I went too.'

'I didn't want to be left behind. I wanted to know what the others were doing.'

Only when study groups have met for the exercise has there been any manifest attempt to account for the composition of other groups. Even then, the comment was:

'Well, it's the same for all of us, we've got used to each other already. We thought it would be easier.'

At one conference in which the number of rooms assigned to the exercise was one less than the number of study groups, those study groups whose rooms were still within bounds immediately occupied them, leaving the deprived study group to sort out its own problems. Though its members were absorbed quite quickly, the difficulties that had been created were smoothed over rather than solved. Later on, in most exercises, when some of the facts of composition have been pointed out, usually by the consultants, there have been attempts to reassemble the total group in plenary session so that the problem of splitting can be studied and, if necessary, a new start made; but these attempts have never, so far, succeeded.

It seems that, having come together, by whatever processes, conscious and unconscious, the groups become so concerned about what might happen in their own groups and what might be going on in other groups that they have to establish some kind of defence forthwith; they have to find a structure. In effect, they accept the members that they have, and proceed immediately to try to establish some kind of organization. They cannot tolerate an examination that would show whether those who have met are those best qualified for the task they have to perform. Any individual who suggests that the composition of the group be subject to scrutiny is always rejected. Since scrutiny of selection inevitably implies looking at criteria for rejection, belief in some magical identification process is necessary in the first anxious minutes. Members are, in reality, faced with the very difficult problem of selecting groups to perform a familiar task – the conduct of intergroup relations – in very unfamiliar circumstances. They have no structure to control the strong feelings that might arise. In this situation they have to act, to take action for action's sake. Usually they act impulsively, clinging to the only structures they have been given – the management 'rules' on the one hand and the existing conference grouping on the other.

At this time groups tend to regard with suspicion any visitors – they may be rejections from other groups, seeking a new group to join. At one conference a member who proposed that the group should study how its members had come together was ignored until he suggested finding out about other groups. He was then sent out, but without any instructions or, indeed, any invitation to return. He wandered from group to group asking the members if they had settled anything, each time expressing the hope that, if they had, he would be allowed to join them.

At the same time visitors, and suspicions about them, may be welcomed as a means of providing distractions from internal problems. The need for some kind of structure is so great that apart from a quick attempt to appoint a chairman and a secretary, little is done other than to discuss machinery for communication. There is usually more talk about sending out representatives to 'communicate' than about internal organization and administration, or even what the communication is to be about. It is not unusual at this stage for the 'elected' officers to find themselves powerless to bring any order into the meeting, and to resign or otherwise cause confusion. If visitors from other groups arrive during this phase they can act as a reproach to the group: other groups have apparently organized themselves. It is usually round about this time that a significant appointment is made, that of 'doorkeeper'. His job is to establish the group boundary and to ensure that some order is introduced into the transactions across it. He greets visitors, inquires their business, and finds out if they can be received. He introduces the 'pause' for thinking in an attempt to reduce the confusion.

In the groups that do take quick initiative one or two voices may be raised to suggest the election of a chairman and a secretary, but leadership is vested in those who want to do something about making contact with other groups. On one occasion – and it is typical – almost as soon as the group assembled a member suggested the sending out of representatives:

'I vote we send out representatives to find out what other groups are doing. Let's see if they know as little as we do.'

He was promptly asked why he didn't go himself. He stood up and moved to the door. As he went he was encouraged to go ahead by most of the group, though it seemed to me, who was consultant on that occasion, that their expressions as they encouraged him were more of relief that somebody was doing something than of positive support for what he was doing. As he reached the door, he paused and asked what he was going as. There was a chorus of 'plenipotentiary'. I commented that that meant he was to do the best he could within the known policy of the group. I wondered if he knew what that was. I added that I had not become aware of any policy and therefore I could only infer that the 'power' given to the plenipotentiary was illusory and that he was being given no sanction at all except to see if other groups knew more than this one. But this one had not even tried to find out what it knew, and hence even the mission was illusory. The representative was halfway through the door. He stopped in his tracks. There was a silence – it seemed long, but was probably only about half a minute:

'If I stop while that is discussed, I'll never get out.'

And with that he went, leaving his group shocked at the way in which it had been led into a course of action without thought or even discussion.

This representative was away for a long time. At first there was an attempt among the remaining members to discuss why they had let him go as they had. This discussion was unproductive and it was not difficult to point out that he had in fact led the group in flight from its task and that, whatever he might say, the real message that he would convey to other groups was precisely this. The group felt a sense of futility; now the representative had gone, there was nothing to do until he got back, but he could not be fetched back because that would weaken his authority, which was, however, still undefined. When he did return he reported on the composition of the three other groups that had been formed, and on the very different receptions he had had from each of them. It soon became clear that some at least of the differences in the way he had been received had been due to his own attitude to the other groups and that, as he became less defensive, because he realized that they were just as confused as his own group, so his reception became more friendly. Nevertheless, the first 'failed act' in adequate communication bedevilled for the rest of the exercise the group's attempts to set up adequate machinery either for its own management or for the management of its relations with other groups.

After the first shock, a major problem that besets most groups is what to communicate about:

'If we knew what to communicate about, we could easily design the machinery for it. The trouble is the task has not been defined. We don't know what we have to do.'

But that they might communicate about their attitudes and feelings for other groups, that they might check their fantasies against such reality as is available to them, takes a long time to be accepted. For to communicate these matters to others they have to acknowledge them to themselves; and that would invite others to comment on them. The early activity – hyper-activity is perhaps a better description – is thus a denial of the task that has been set. Moreover, it can be seen that pre-occupation with setting up machinery for communication and with sending out representatives to follow undefined or ill-defined policies is, in reality, a means of dealing with the group's own internal problems. It is an attempt to project confusion and doubts about potency onto others. The selection, or self-selection, of representatives in the early sessions is also, of course, a means of removing those who are not easily integrated into an inactive, though probably thoughtful, group.

While uncertainty about internal problems, projected upon the staff as inadequate task definition or inadequately stated rules, makes policy about communication difficult to formulate, it becomes noticeable that those visitors from other groups who come with a specific purpose have little difficulty in taking over the missing group leadership. No amount of protest about 'courtesy to a visitor' can obscure the willingness with which the visitor is allowed to dominate the meeting.

Most groups only gradually come to accept this view of their behaviour, but as they do, they begin to develop some kind of organization that is at least sufficiently secure to permit them to lower their barriers to ideas from other groups, and even to think of changes in membership; or at least of the formation of new groups made up of some members from groups previously formed. So far, however, agreement to do something as a total membership has seldom been more than verbal. Whenever representatives of all groups in a meeting of representatives have proposed definite action, however mild, there have been objections from the groups left behind. Even when agreement was reached by representatives, and confirmed by their own groups, that the representatives should meet with the staff at the centre to exchange views about each other's behaviour, and presumably about the staff's behaviour as well, action was somehow delayed – by questions about procedure, by mistakes about time – until there was no time left in the exercise to implement it.

On one occasion, when the members split into two groups, their representatives finally agreed that they all wanted to reconstitute a plenary session and take the staff to task, not only for the conduct of the exercise, but for the timing of events in the conference and for the quality of the lectures that had been given to them. They were just about to achieve this – one group had actually reached the centre – when it was discovered that a splinter group had been formed, which wanted and achieved a reopening of the negotiations. These lasted until the end of the exercise.

In general, agreed plans seldom lead to any action. The important lessons concern the difficulty of taking any action while divergent views exist; the virtual impossibility of getting unanimity on anything except rejection of what is not in the group; and the ease with which one person, provided he is from outside, knows what he wants, and is determined to get it, can take over the leadership of a group. The only unanimity is in the unsconcious collusion to get on with internal affairs and to resist by all possible means – and there are many – intrusion of the external environment.

THE ROLE OF CONSULTANT TO A GROUP

On only one occasion has any consultant been left unemployed for the whole exercise. There were a number of possible explanations for this isolated occurrence. The consultant concerned was the only one, on that occasion, who was also a consultant to a study group. The members' behaviour could have been an act of hostility to her as a study-group consultant, a symbolic rejection of study groups, or an attempt to avoid putting her in another role and thus endangering her 'goodness' as a study-group leader. There was no evidence in the exercise to suggest which it was, or, rather, there was so much evidence for each of these possibilities that they were probably all true in varying degrees.

Except for this instance, all the staff members made available as consultants have been called on, though there have been delays, and in two exercises one group has met for most of the time without consultant help. At all times consultants have had to be aware of the reality of the demand for their help. When they have been unsure that the decision to call them in has been a real one, they have questioned the sanction for their presence, and sometimes have left while the group has made up its mind.

An important dynamic that is introduced into the exercise by the fact that some, but not all, of the staff are available as consultants to groups, is a built-in incentive to members to split the staff group. At the same time, however, they are facing themselves with the possibility that the consultant may not be helpful to them but may consciously or unconsciously sabotage their efforts to unite in opposition to the staff. The consultant has always to be aware of the ambivalence with which he or she is regarded, and of the temptation to secede from the staff group that will be offered. He will also be aware, however, that if he succumbs to this temptation, his usefulness to the group will thereby be limited. Capture, however attractive to the group and to the consultant, inevitably negates his capacity to provide opportunities to learn about intergroup relations, since this involves his being at least sufficiently detached from group affairs to be able to explain some of the frustrating phenomena that occur. More importantly, perhaps, capture of a consultant by any group calls into question the effectiveness of the whole staff group, and hence the stability and dependability of conference management. Its stability and dependability may indeed be questionable, but to question them safely a group needs support from the other groups as well, and that involves making appropriate relations with other groups.

Consultants have greater difficulty in dealing with the group's desire to treat the exercise as an extension of the study-group experience. If a group has to come to terms with its own identity and with its own internal relations and organization as a prerequisite of effective communication with other groups, then there is reality in the need to sort out internal problems. To study interaction there has to be some interaction, and to achieve coherent interaction there has to be some kind of internal structure. In this sense the consultant should help with the sorting out of internal relations and the setting up of the necessary organization. But whereas in the study group he is concerned only with the internal life of the group, in the intergroup exercise he is concerned with it in relation to the external environment, and hence his interventions are bound to be different. The difference is that in the study group the consultant is concerned only with what is happening 'here and now'; in the exercise he is concerned with the 'here and now' in relation to the 'there and then'. Because unless there is a member of another group actually present, information about other groups, whose relations with his own group are his concern, must always be based partially on reports of what has happened somewhere else.

One consequence is that it is difficult for the consultant to avoid standing on one side, making comments on the effectiveness or ineffectiveness of the behaviour of the group. He can thus appear even more omniscient, and unhelpful, than a study-group consultant. He is not as personally exposed as other members of the group, and certainly not as personally exposed as he is in the study group. Whenever I have been consultant to a group – and I believe this feeling is shared to some extent by my colleagues – the ease with which, as an outsider, I can point to ineffectiveness and ineptitude, without being exposed to the same sort of test myself, tends to inhibit my attempts to help members to understand the problems with which they are faced. They can, and do of course, attack the staff group and my interpretation of the staff role, but I have an external referent that is politically well organized to fall back on, and it is not just my personal competence that is under close scrutiny.

Nevertheless, a member of the staff who is designated as a consultant to a group, and yet remains a member of the staff group responsible for the exercise, is put in a difficult position. The staff group frequently tries to find a more simple solution. It is not unusual, for example, for the staff to suggest that those who are consultants should cease to be a part of the management. But it seems improbable that that kind of separation would work; members would not believe that the consultant was not part of the staff group, and the staff group would be in collusion with the members to split itself right down the middle. The dilemma does not seem unlike that of any board of directors or other group with collective responsibility for an institution, whose members also take managerial or professional roles within it. As members of the group they carry a joint responsibility for leadership of the whole; as individuals they are responsible for their own management or professional function. The two roles are often in conflict, and compromise or resignation may be the only possible outcomes.

THE STAFF GROUP

What is left of the staff group stays in its own 'territory'. It too has its own consultant (one of its own number) whose job is to help the staff group to learn about its own intergroup relations. The staff group makes members available as consultants, who, when they are in other groups, are plenipotentiaries in that they are vested with full powers to do what they can, within the rules laid down for the exercise, in the circumstances in which they find themselves. So far, the staff group has never recalled those it has so sent out. It has sent out delegates with instructions to inform other groups about management's views, and observers to find out what is happening. But for the most part, having made consultants available, those left behind have remained passive, waiting for groups or representatives of groups to visit them. When that has happened the consultant to the staff group acts as consultant to the intergroup meeting.

The first visits, apart from those to request the help of a consultant, are usually for clarification, to ask questions about the rules of the exercise. Though some groups are confused about what they have been told at the opening, and their questions have some reality, there is invariably behind the questions some test-out of staff intentions and integrity. In the early stages the staff are usually put in the position of saying 'no' to requests – to negotiate about a party, to extend the number of available rooms, and so on. Saying 'no' can itself be reassuring, because it implies that complete anarchy will not prevail – at least one group knows what it will not do. It also makes it easier for members to say 'no' to the staff and thus to test, in a valid way, what will happen if they defy authority.

An implication that frequently becomes stronger as the exercise goes on is that the staff have 'fixed' the whole exercise and can therefore predict what will happen. Though I have given here of necessity a generalized account of the intergroup exercise, the staff never know in advance what will happen, or when, on any given occasion. But the implication is that the staff are all engaged in a conspiracy to produce a predetermined result. Within this reasoning the director does not need to be told anything: he knows, and what is more, he knows in advance. Yet members also know that if the director behaved as if he knew what was going to happen and when, then he could be out-manoeuvred by clever members and hence could be destroyed. His destruction would then prove that the exercise, and the conference, were based on false theories and false hypotheses and need not be taken seriously.

Perhaps one of the odd things about the exercise is how seriously it is taken. Members frequently express amazement at this themselves. The exercise is a charade, a game, yet as they play it members seriously question the staff's qualifications and rights to expose them not only to the exercise, but to the conference as a whole. By such questioning they can deny, or attempt to deny, that work, hard and painful work, is required if the problems of leading and following are to be understood. Such questioning can also be used to obscure the anxieties that arise from the inability to tolerate uncertainty about task performance. There are few work groups which are uninterested in success, and if criteria for measuring success are difficult to lay down – as in any exercise for learning by experience they must be – toleration of uncertainty is bound to be severely tested. The danger is that intolerance can lead to a change of task definition in an attempt to find more measurable criteria.

In an intergroup exercise the staff are in constant danger of imagining that they are managing an exercise for its own sake; that is, that they are managing a communication system, but not necessarily a learning process. The staff feel impotent when nothing appears to be happening and rapidly get to the stage at which they want to take action, if only to relieve their own anxiety. Part of the way through one exercise the staff could not see that anything was being achieved; they became so anxious that they even started to take decisions about the strategy of future exercises. They found themselves discussing what they would do or would not do the next time. In their fear that they had made a mess of the current exercise – before it was over – they comforted themselves with anticipation of success in the next. But this behaviour of course denied their task of helping members to learn from the current exercise, and had they persisted they might easily have taken unwarranted decisions about the future.

Typically, in practice the amount of information reaching the staff group is sparse, and what little is reported is usually trivial. Representatives of groups, on their way to visit other groups, sometimes call on the staff group to tell the director to which group they are going; occasionally they tell him why; and, still more rarely, on their way back they say what the result has been. It appears to be assumed that though the director need not be told anything important, he should be told all that is un-important. He needs, in other words, to be treated with respect and consideration, and a way of doing this is to propitiate him with token gifts. Behind the respect and consideration, however, is the hope that providing him with useless information may keep him from finding out anything useful; and hence make it easier to discredit him. The major communications to management are inferential; they have to be deduced not from what is said, but largely from what is not said.

Perhaps the most important inferential communication has been mentioned above: that what members want to use the exercise for is to examine whether it does provide opportunities to learn about leadership. Inevitably, they become preoccupied with conference and exercise leadership. The intergroup exercise is the one event in which the primary task invites them to examine, in detail, their relations with the staff as a whole and the internal relations of the staff group – the leadership élite of the conference. In the large group members are faced by consultants, and even if one of these is the conference director they do not meet management as management. They may discuss conference leadership and management, but that is not the task of the event. The only other events in which they meet the staff, and hence management, as a group, are the opening and ending plenaries. The former is too early and the latter too late for real work on member-staff relations. In the exercise, however, they find that for some reason it is difficult to attack exercise leadership directly, as a total group, even with assistance from staff as consultants. They can only attack indirectly by cutting leadership off from evidence of what is going on.

It is never easy to analyse adequately the reasons for the fear of direct attack. At one level it can be suggested that there is no agreement among members that an attack is desirable. There are real but varied opinions about the effectiveness of both exercise and conference. At another level, the hurry to get out of the room at the beginning could suggest that as a potential enemy the staff are felt to be too powerful. The acceptance of some staff as consultants to groups shows that this feeling does not apply to individuals on the staff because the same phenomena occur whoever are nominated as director or consultants. It is the roles and not the persons who are feared.

In one exercise, I arrived at the place that the staff group was to occupy about a minute before a session was due to start. I found it occupied by a group of members. As I entered there was a laugh and, turning to me, one member said:

'Well, we've taken over your territory, what are you going to do about that?'

I glanced at the clock and replied:

'Nothing now, because the session hasn't started. But in about half a minute, when it does, I shall try at least to understand what is happening and I expect I'll make an interpretation about it.'

But by the time the session started there was nobody left to make an interpretation to.

Outside the exercise the members often succeed in much they have been trying to do within it. They certainly succeed in splitting the staff, in particular in setting consultants against their own headquarters. As director I am frequently taken noisily to task by my colleagues for the 'impossible' position into which I have put them, either by my words or manner in the opening, or by my replies to representatives who have visited me. Dr Turquet, when he directed an exercise, complained that everybody out in the groups appeared to know just what was happening, whereas he was not told anything by the groups, and even his colleagues only confused him. At the time I was acting as consultant to a group and had been feeling that he was getting much more information than my colleagues ever gave me when I was director!

Nevertheless, a consultant on his return to the staff group is faced by two problems. The first is the real difficulty of giving a brief appreciation of a confused situation, and the second is his need to get his confusion out of himself. A catalogue of events, an account of who said what and when – the gossip – is often fascinating, but it leaves the recipient to make his own appreciation of the situation before he can make sound decisions; and if the decisions have to be made quickly the need to listen to so much content – however interesting – can be exasperating. On the other hand, consultants who have been bewildered by what has been happening in the group in which they have been working, and who are, in consequence, uncertain about their own performance, need to have somebody to whom they can unburden themselves. The incompatibility of these two needs – of the director for an appreciation, and of the consultant to 'externalize' his confusion – can add to the staff-group difficulties in making decisions about what action is best to further members' learning opportunities.

Certainly as director of the exercise I often feel that I do not need to be told about members' behaviour. I have only to observe staff behaviour. That epitomizes what is happening in the exercise. The technical problem, as yet unsolved, is that these observations, which are so informative, are often made outside the time and territory of the exercise and not within it. Perhaps this is inevitable since the whole conference is, in one sense, one large intergroup exercise mediated through a series of events. In other words, though the primary tasks of the different events are different, each event, apart from the intergroup exercise, has as its secondary task the examination of the model of leadership and management as demonstrated by the staff group.

THE ENDING OF THE EXERCISE

The intergroup exercise ends with a plenary session. This session is opened by the director giving a review of what he has observed in his role, and reporting the inferences he has drawn from his observations. His statement is followed by discussion among staff and members. The exercise, unlike other 'here and now' events, is concluded by a review because its nature splits members into different groups and hence no one person can have an overall view of what has happened. Learning takes place in all member groups and in the staff group, and not just in a member's own group.

The director's review gives a chronological account of the main events of the exercise, and a commentary on the interpretations that were made at the time. It concludes with a brief overall interpretation of the reasons for these events. The purpose is to try to present the data coherently and in a pattern which relates cause and effect. The overall interpretation is given as an example of some of the learning that might be articulated. So far as I am able I discuss the pattern of staff relationships and the changes that have occurred as a result of members' impact on them:

'. . . By this time, more than an hour had passed. The staff began to feel paranoid. There had been no requests for help. Clearly the consultants who had been offered were not wanted. We began to consider whether we should take some action. We were responsible for the exercise and it was unpalatable to think that we were not wanted and that we could not do anything. In the event what we did was to quarrel about our social behaviour. Some of us by this time had got ourselves drinks from the bar, and some members of the staff questioned our ethics in drinking during the working session. Though voices were raised and the quarrel became acrimonious, there did not feel to be very much reality in it, and directing attention to what it symbolized, that is, the attempt to split the staff group, dealt with it for the time being, albeit somewhat uneasily.'

'. . . By this time only the secretary and myself were left at staff headquarters. I had nothing left to do but take her out for a drink – which I did. The serious point was the extent to which, by having delegated all jobs to other members of the staff, I had rendered myself impotent by abdication. On reflection I felt that I had not so much abdicated as given myself the problem of how long I would leave them without trying to find out what they were doing. I felt as though I had eight parts of myself scattered round the building and had constantly to reassure myself that they were all doing what I would have done had I been there.'

I hope that such disclosures, like the overall interpretation, will encourage members to examine the behaviour of their own groups in a similar way, and hence help them to become aware of similar experiences in other groups and meetings outside the conference.

CHAPTER 8

Application Groups

The purpose of application groups is to explore the potential relevance of conference learning to normal working situations. Members choose the material to be studied. A consultant attached to each application group tries to help members to look at the case material produced in the light of conference experience. Application groups are therefore composed of those doing the same or similar jobs in their ordinary work. In contrast to study groups, application groups are as homogeneous as possible.

We have found the application group to be among the more difficult events to conduct. Technically, it should be the easiest. Members of staff who have a clinical background are familiar with the case-conference method of teaching, and those with an educational background are accustomed to tutorial groups and to seminar-type events. Some of the difficulty arises from the problem of articulating conference learning, and hence of finding ways in which it can be applied. Some arises from the conference institution in which the application group occurs. Even when members of the staff have attempted to use more than conference learning by adding special knowledge or experience of their own about the problems being discussed, there has seldom been the spontaneity that would be expected in more traditional educational institutions.

EARLIER FORMS OF APPLICATION GROUP

In the 1957 conference (Trist and Sofer, 1959), each application group was given a project, outside the conference, as a part of its case material. Thus an application group composed of members with an educational background visited the Leicester Education Authority to discuss the Leicestershire experiment in the transfer from primary to secondary education, an innovation of national importance in view of the controversy over the eleven-plus tests; a group concerned with penal institutions and

114

delinquency visited the Leicester Police to examine and discuss the selection and promotion scheme that had recently been instituted; one industrial group visited a company that had been running a successful experiment in industrial co-partnership for some years; and another visited the government training and rehabilitation centre.

In subsequent conferences external projects were dropped. The visits were not easy to arrange. They involved much administrative work, agreeing times and dates of meetings, arranging for return visits of personnel from the various bodies or companies concerned in the projects, and preparing the material that was to be used in the conference. In addition, the introduction of a large number of the conference members into external organizations and of representatives from external organizations into the conference further complicated interpersonal and intergroup relationships already sufficiently complicated. But, most importantly, we felt that neither the staff nor the members could do adequate justice to the host institutions in the midst of all the other things that were going on in a short conference. We did not feel that our hosts were adequately repaid for the time they spent and the trouble they took to display their problems and their attempted solutions. It seemed that, faced with the need to make some contribution, neither staff nor members could do other than applaud indiscriminately or appear destructively critical. There was too little time to make the constructively critical study that might have both helped conference learning and repaid the host institution for its exposure and hospitality.

In practice, the projects were intrusions into the conference process, though members of some application groups were impressed and moved by what they had seen and heard (Trist and Sofer, 1959). In those groups the project dominated subsequent application-group sessions to the exclusion of what was happening elsewhere in the conference. In others, in which the project did not 'take', it was experienced as a distraction. The idea behind the projects was sound: to provide members of application groups with case material that was the same for all of them, and was relevant to their own jobs. But such projects need far more time than could be given in the conference or by the host institutions. It may be possible to reintroduce them when conference methods are extended and introduced into longer training programmes.

At subsequent conferences attempts were made to get application groups to follow a predetermined routine: to take a problem census; to search for a theme; to identify problems within the theme; to survey available cases to determine their appropriateness to the explication of identified problems; and then to make formal presentation of the case material prior to discussion. While this technique did, to some extent, make it easier to put into words what had been discussed and what had been learnt during application-group sessions, neither technique nor learning was intrinsically consistent with, or even relevant to, the rest of the conference. The sessions were too often additions to, and outside, conference experience. Not only members but staff as well felt too constrained by the technique.

At various conferences the place of application groups in the programme has been changed. At one conference we tried putting application groups as the first working event, immediately following the opening session. It was hoped that, since members came to the conference from their own jobs, application groups would provide a familiar connection between job and conference. It was also hoped that the homogeneity of application groups would help members to feel more at home than if they were put into the heterogeneous study groups straight away. It soon became clear, however, that on arrival at the conference members were far more concerned about study groups than they were about application groups. In these conferences the early application-group sessions were largely wasted; members were impatient to get into study groups. It was as though, having dealt with their anxiety sufficiently to apply for membership and subsequently to arrive, they wanted to get on with what they felt to be the most significant conference experience. Application groups now start late in the programme, and the programme ends with them.

THE PRIMARY TASK OF APPLICATION GROUPS

The primary task of application groups is to consider the application of conference learning to members' normal work. Performance of this task must of necessity relate what has happened and is happening in the conference to the external environment. It involves therefore two other subtasks: some assessment of conference learning and a preparation for return to the real world outside. Application groups are thus a major part of the conference 'export' process.

The problem of fitting application groups into the total conference pattern is as yet not fully solved. Most members find application groups both a relief from the intensive and unusual methods of the rest of the conference and, at the same time, a disappointment and a let-down after other experience. Those members who want to continue with study-group, large-group, and intergroup experience inevitably seek to turn the application groups into one or the other and try to trap their consultant into going into collusion with them. Consultants to application groups have sometimes been accused by members of leaning over backwards to avoid turning them into study groups to such an extent that they have diminished their value even as application groups. As against this, those consultants who have unwittingly colluded with members to change the task of their application groups have found that, though at first both they and the members have felt a greater satisfaction with their meetings, they have faced an almost insoluble problem when bringing the group to an end. They have had no means of getting out of the situation other than by an exchange of compliments and thanks, an exchange that both know to be a denial of reality.

In the plenary reviews there have been members who have protested strongly against the flatness of the application groups as compared with the other small-group activity, the study group. There have equally been those who have welcomed the flatness as a means of giving them time to prepare themselves for returning to the more ordinary world of work. Holders of both views experience the application groups as unexciting when compared with other conference events. Application groups, as part of the export process, have to provide an opportunity to deal with the mixture of depression, elation, and anxiety that accompanies the loss of what have become valued human experiences. They are intended to deal with the let-down within the conference rather than leave it all until after the conference is over, when members have neither each other nor the staff to help them. It may well be that without the experience of flatness application groups could not accomplish this part of their task, and that this inevitably begets a sense of frustration in the attempt to articulate and apply conference learning.

The staff share both the depression and the frustration, but in the application groups have not readily to hand, as in the study groups, the techniques for dealing with them as group phenomena, and the problem of maximizing the learning opportunity of the mixed feelings remains.

Perhaps it is even more important that the work of application groups conveys unmistakably that what has been learnt, if anything, does not automatically solve all the problems raised; that, however intensive the experience of conference learning, however firm the conviction that much has been learnt, only new ways of looking at problems, not solutions, have been offered. Any lingering belief that earlier conference experience would magically provide solutions to problems previously thought intractable is, in the application groups, dispelled. What has to be learnt is that, even with new approaches, most human problems, and particularly those of leading and managing, still require hard work; and even then some of them will be insoluble, or it will not be possible to implement the solution.

My own view is that we should try a different order of priority in the tasks of the application group, and that we should define the primary task as the accomplishment of the export process. Application groups would then be less concerned with case material produced by members, and the emphasis would be on conference ending. In our present programme the large-group event is finished before the application-group event begins, the intergroup exercise is almost over, and the end of the study groups is in sight. Ending is the current preoccupation of members and staff alike. The application of conference learning to this process would have considerable value for its own sake. In this sense it could use case material produced by members from their own working backgrounds, but case material from the 'there and then' of the conference would also be relevant. The danger would be that the transfer of conference learning to other external situations would be largely by analogy. Staff acting as consultants to application groups might have to be prepared to produce more material themselves, and do more teaching from it. This would place a considerable burden on staff and I am not sure that it is one that can be adequately carried.

CONTENT OF APPLICATION-GROUP DISCUSSIONS

Even at the end of a conference, many members still appear to be in difficulties, and are sometimes distressed about getting an intellectual grasp of what the conference has been about. This is epitomized by the demand, that used to be made so frequently, that the staff should help members to prepare a report about the conference that they can take back to their own organizations.

'I've spent a lot of time here and my company has paid a lot of money for me to come. They're not going to be very pleased when all I can tell them is that I've had an interesting experience. They didn't give me the time and pay the money for that.'

Now that a large number of conferences have been held and more members of the same organizations have attended, this demand is less insistent than it was at the beginning. Nevertheless, a number of those who come to conferences are expected, on their return, to make a report to their colleagues or superiors, and this they find difficult.

It is perhaps not surprising, therefore, that towards the end of a conference some members are concerned to get something practical and specific out of it that has immediate application in their own organizations, even if it is only a kind of second-hand consultation on a current problem. In earlier conferences, 'special interest' sessions tried to satisfy this demand. On some occasions we have introduced special events such as role-playing, panel discussion, and other training techniques. Though such techniques are valid methods of training in their own right, and though material thrown up at the conference was used in the events given to them, we now feel that as events they were out of keeping with the rest of the conference. Their primary task was to demonstrate a technique of training for the sake of the technique and hence they did not fit into the pattern of a conference that was designed for a different purpose. This does not mean that such techniques cannot be and are not introduced into application groups whenever their use helps to illuminate the problem being discussed; but they are then introduced for the sake of the problem, not for the sake of the technique.

In the same way, the conference structure and culture can themselves serve as case material. The consistencies and inconsistencies in its structure, culture, and task can throw useful light on the problems the conference is called upon to study; not, again it should be emphasized, to try to teach conference design for its own sake, since that is not the purpose of the conference, but to illustrate the problems of fitting structure and culture to a task; similarly, staff behaviour can illustrate some of the problems of taking different kinds of leadership roles.

An application group usually starts with a definition of its task by the consultant. This is followed by an invitation to the members to consider possible subjects for discussion. At this stage the consultant encourages members to look at a number of topics that may be relevant to the learning of the conference, and discourages the too premature production of a 'case'. This phase, which may last for two or more sessions, is intended to deal with some of the problems of the transition to a new way of working, and to give time for a general look at the similarities and differences in members' experience and background.

It is usual at this stage for members to ask to change their application group. They have been assigned to these groups as a result of information they have given on their registration forms. But it is sometimes difficult to be sure from the information given that members have sufficient in common to form a relatively homogeneous group; and furthermore, in practice, members may feel that they belong elsewhere. Though we recognize that some of the requests for a change may be due less to the unsuitabliity of the allocation than to the acting-out of other problems of relationship, arrangements for transfer can be made with the mutual consent of the groups concerned.

By the second, third, or fourth session some member of the group will present a detailed case history of a management, organizational, or professional problem from his own work, and this is then discussed until the group decides to change to some other case. The first cases produced are not infrequently stories of success, or, at most, of only minor difficulty. Members are wary of exposing their real problems to scrutiny. In this they are of course affected by the composition of the groups. With the best will in the world it is not possible to avoid building into some application groups external hostilities or rivalries of which staff are ignorant. Even when attention is drawn to them it is not always possible to make other arrangements. Industrial or commercial competition can usually, though not always, be avoided; but ill feeling between, for example, a teacher training college and a university institute of education may be not only unknown to the staff, but not even disclosed in the conference until an application group that contains members of both has been meeting for some time.

Material produced for discussion is also affected by the relative status of the members of a group. Job titles and necessarily brief descriptions of duties are notoriously ambiguous means of identification and unreliable guides to the responsibility carried and authority exercised. Too wide differences in status can introduce difficulties in relationship that may inhibit members' willingness to expose either themselves or their own organizations. Ideally, conference members would be recruited through their anticipated homogeneous application-group membership – but, so far, in the particular conferences I am describing this has not proved possible; it is noticeable that in other conferences with which we have been concerned and in which membership has been limited to one main source –

industry, education, or the church – application groups have been easier.

In some conferences particular application groups are faced with trying to help one of their members with a specific and urgent problem. In one, a member heard, halfway through the conference, that in his absence a major company reorganization had been announced. So far as he could tell the repercussions of this would drastically change his own job, cut down his responsibility, and destroy much of his authority. He decided not to return home at once but to ask his application group to help him with his return. The reasons for the reorganization were discussed, the new organization was studied, and two sessions were devoted to role-playing his anticipated meetings with his colleagues and chairman. In the role-playing he took each role in turn, including his own, and other members of the group took his role. Many months later he expressed considerable gratitude to the other members of the group for the help he had had in coping with a particularly difficult period in his work. Such incidents and opportunities are fortunately rare. The more usual case material is about the everyday problems of managerial and professional life.

THE ROLE OF CONSULTANT

The task of consultant to an application group is defined as assisting members to relate conference learning to their normal work. His job is to relate knowledge that has been available to members in the conference to the case material they produce; and hence to avoid, as far as possible, introducing other special knowledge or experience. In other words, we now feel that it is not appropriate for a consultant with special knowledge to contribute that knowledge – unless there have been opportunities in the conference for the members to acquire it also.

For these reasons consultants to application groups are chosen, not for their special knowledge of the field represented by the members of the application group, but for their ability to help the application group to which they are assigned. By this device we hope, first, that consultants will be, to some extent, protected from becoming 'experts' on content; and, second, that two-way communication will be improved. Application-group members have to teach consultants about their own field, about the skill required and the conditions in which it can be exercised. The consultant can then help to demonstrate how insights obtainable in the conference can be used to illuminate the problems raised. He brings to bear his experience of groups to help the group to work as a group, and his experience of relationships to throw light on the relationship problems in the cases presented.

Such, at least, is the theory on which we are working at present, but it would be idle to pretend that we are very satisfied with the results. First, the insights that the consultant gets from a conference are different from those that the members get, because he observes from a different point of view; second, as consultants attend a number of conferences they inevitably become familiar with most of the fields of work represented by the members; and third, the familiarity they thus acquire is based only on second- or third-hand experience, and is not, therefore, necessarily helpful either to the consultant or to the members. The dilemma is not easy to resolve. On the one hand, if a consultant contributes his own special knowledge – for example, if a psychiatrist contributes psychiatric knowledge to a discussion about executive counselling in an application group composed of production managers – he is inevitably led into didactic teaching of a subject that is not a part of the conference task; on the other hand, if a consultant has no experience of the work of the members, either they have to spend most of the time teaching him, or he will be tempted into making superficial and oversimplified general contributions.

One learning opportunity is provided by the behaviour of the consultant in his leading of the application group. And an important aspect of this leadership is the demonstration of the use of insight into group processes to help the task of the group, without turning the application group into a study group. The application group is a 'there and then' learning event, not a 'here and now', and the consultant has to demonstrate how to use insight into the 'here and now' without exceeding his terms of reference or assuming a sanction to explore private feelings that he has not been given. A potentially dangerous implication of study- and large- group experience is that whenever the performance of a committee or other working group is inhibited by the rivalries, envies, and hostilities inherent in the interpersonal and intergroup relationships of its members, these feelings should be exposed and 'worked through'. But in ordinary working groups there is seldom any sanction for the exposure of one's own, let alone other people's, feelings and attitudes. All that is permissible is the use of insight into the state of the group as a guide to one's own behaviour.

CHAPTER 9

The Plenary Sessions

The plenary sessions consist of the conference opening, the lectures, and what we have so far called the conference reviews, though we now doubt if that is the correct title for them.

The first conference in 1957 recognized the principle that conferences designed to provide members with opportunities to learn about the interpersonal and intergroup problems of leadership must provide for their full participation in the conference process. Even so, in retrospect, I now feel that the traditional expectation of regular plenaries, for work or social activities, led us to include more plenaries in the programme than were required for conference task performance. One consequence was that in planning subsequent conferences there was confusion about both the task and the timing of plenary sessions and indeed about the need for members to meet at regular intervals. At times it has seemed that the primary task of some plenaries has been to allow members to meet for the sake of meeting, and that it has therefore been the staff's job to find them something to meet about.

The introduction of the large-group event for the study of large-group behaviour has, to some extent, removed this need. We have been freed to give more attention to the purpose of various kinds of plenary session. At one stage we almost decided to experiment with a conference that had none. A number of the lessons that were learnt in earlier conferences have now been clarified and, as in other events, some of them that were lost in subsequent experiments have been relearnt.

The 1957 conference was opened by an address of welcome from the Vice Chancellor of the University of Leicester; this was followed by the conference chairman's explaining administrative and residential arrangements, and conducting a tour of the buildings. A second session was then given to a technical description of the conference by the programme director. The first of these sessions lasted two hours, and the second, after tea, for an hour and a half. At the time no one had a clear idea of what could be communicated at this stage and how best to communicate it.

'The original plan had been to hold the first Study Group sessions at 4.30 p.m. This was found to allow too little time for introduction and they were postponed until after dinner. There was some evidence that this period of waiting, short though it was, increased the tension to some degree inevitable in anticipation of an unknown experience' (Trist and Sofer, 1959).

It was found subsequently that very little had been communicated by this form of opening. Since then many different kinds of opening have been tried, including the sending out of far more explanatory literature in advance of the actual opening session. If we judge from what members say during the conference, none has succeeded in communicating with any reality what the conference is about, and, as I have said, there have been suggestions of abandoning any attempt at a formal beginning.

THE CONFERENCE OPENING

Nevertheless, the first event of a conference does mark a change in status for both members and staff. Up to that moment, the conference has been a plan, a paper exercise. As soon as it starts, experience begins. Conference membership is the only characteristic that is common to all members and the only thing that unites them. They have left their normal jobs to come to the conference at the invitation of the conference sponsors; their only identification with the conference is through their membership; and the only way in which that can be given corporate realization is by a meeting of all. We have therefore kept the first session as a plenary. But since we do not expect to communicate much at this stage, we have reduced it to what is, in effect, a ritual.

Even as a ritual, however, it still has to have a meaning. In the first session, therefore, the director gives a formal welcome to the members, introduces the staff (who are with him on the platform), gives the conference secretary the opportunity to make any administrative announcements, and then makes a brief statement about what is to happen. This last is a slight amplification of the brochure that members have already received. Questions are then invited. Experience has shown that the questions, if any, are largely of the 'test-out' kind; that is to say, that it is not the questioners' intention only to elicit information, but also to find out if the staff are properly prepared. The questions are usually administrative:

'May we borrow books from the library?'

'Will lecturers provide papers or notes of their lectures or do we have to take our own?'

and so on. All these questions are treated factually and if possible answered. If we do not know the answer we say so, and set in motion means of finding out. No attempt is made to interpret the meaning of the questions or the reasons for their being asked.

When we first introduced this kind of opening session, we allowed a normal period of one and a half hours. There were so few questions, however, sometimes none at all, that short of stimulating discussion artificially or anticipating the large-group event there seemed nothing to do but close it early. We now allow only half an hour for the opening plenary and have found this adequate so far. We recognize, however, that announcing on the programme that the session will be so short discourages questions, and the time allowance may have to be changed if a future director changes the kind of opening I have used. The important points to be achieved during the opening are that the conference secretary, whose job during the conference is to look after members, should make herself known, should let her voice be heard, and that members shortly to go into study groups should be able to identify their consultants.

No attempt is made to reassure members about the experiences they might be anticipating. What reassurance there is, if any, is in a demonstration that the staff, as represented by the director and the secretary, know what *they* are going to do. Nor is there any attempt to tell members what they ought to get from the conference. In Bion's terms: members arriving at a conference are inevitably dependent upon the organizers for organizing it; therefore the appropriate basic assumption to be mobilized for an opening event is dependence; and for this the leader has to show himself dependable. This is what I try to do as conference director; and by my conduct of the session I try to display the relationship between the various roles the staff will play and my own.

My colleagues and some members have sometimes felt that I make my statement almost too flat and impersonal; that there is a bit too much of a 'this is it – take it or leave it' attitude. When I look back on the various opening sessions I have conducted I am conscious that I have intended to provide members with a last opportunity for withdrawal before they become involved in the conference process, and the way I behave could suggest that I am advising anybody who has doubts about his attendance to leave at once. An implication of these accusations is that I do too little to help the members to settle down, that I leave them too anxious about what is to happen next. There may well be truth in these comments, but I am not sure that I know any other way of avoiding the greater dangers: on the one hand of going on too long in an attempt to communicate a full description of conference events, and hence of raising anxiety unbearably; or, on the other, of giving false reassurances that make it more difficult for members to accept the reality of the study-group experience that follows, and, more importantly, the integrity of staff intention.

Immediately after the opening, tea, or if the time is different, some other appropriate drink, is served, and then within half an hour the first study-group session takes place.

<h2>THE LECTURE SERIES</h2>

Lectures, as has been said, are primarily to give the theoretical framework on which the overall design and events of the conference are based. We are not concerned with conference design for its own sake, but with the articulation of the concepts of behaviour that have contributed to the design. Lectures are offered on theories of individual and group behaviour, and on organization. Other lectures give examples of the application of the theories to practical problems within the lecturers' own experience. As far as possible each lecture is timed to take place when members are preoccupied with its subject-matter. The intention is to offer the theoretical framework appropriate to the move through the conference process. The timing is decided in advance. Though it would be possible to adjust the order and to put in different lectures if we found the timing wrong in practice, we would then have to face the problems that would arise from a change in the programme, on which members depend for some of their security. So far, we have adhered to the programme.

The lectures, however, have a second purpose: to provide a familiar form of teaching in what is otherwise an unfamiliar, and for most people in the United Kingdom a strange, experience. By giving lectures we hope to demonstrate both that it is possible to use lectures in such a setting and, at the same time, that purely intellectual devices have limitations when it comes to learning about emotional experiences. Members find lectures reassuring, not only because they are familiar with the method but also because they have the opportunity to meet the staff in traditional academic roles; thus they have a kind of standard by which to judge the staff's performance in the less familiar roles in other events. The lectures, in other words, provide a familiar baseline for judgements about unfamiliar experiences.

The lectures are staged as academic events. There is no chairman to mediate between, or to control, lecturer and audience; the lecturer is on the platform on his own, and conducts his own discussion after he has finished speaking. This arrangement is possible because there are never outside lecturers, for whom symbolic institutional sanction in the form of a chairman would have to be given. Lecturers are members of the staff, who, in other events, take other roles. The choice of lecturers, and hence of subjects, is thus limited and there are variations in the lecture series from conference to conference. Our experience of visiting lecturers, however competent as lecturers, has been that they find it difficult to attune themselves to the mood of their audience. Members' experience in other parts of the conference makes them demand much of their lecturers, particularly in the discussion that follows the lecture. As a minimum they expect familiarity with the life of the conference.

From experience of lecturing at these conferences the audience could be described as critical but attentive. In the 1957 conference we did not expect the lectures to be particularly well attended. We thought they would be treated like university lectures, attendance depending both on the subject and on the reputation of the lecturer. But at that conference the attendance was virtually complete; and at all subsequent conferences the same thing has happened. To be a lecturer is in my experience always worrying, but I have found, and other lecturers have reported the same feeling, that lecturing in the setting of the conferences has always been unusually stimulating. In particular, lecturers have found that the other events in the conference, being so vivid in the minds of the members, have supplied such apt illustrations of what the lecture is about that understanding between audience and lecturer has been easy to achieve.

THE PLENARY REVIEWS

Because, at the end of the conference, members return to their ordinary jobs, and application groups are closest in texture to normal working, application groups provide the most fitting ending to the conference. At the same time, by the end of the conference, members have had experience of many different kinds of small- and large-group activity and have made different kinds of relationship with each other, and with the staff in various roles. Most members have to some extent developed feelings and attitudes, both for and against, the conference as a whole and the events in it. By that time the conference has meaning for them as an institution. Plenary reviews are intended to provide an opportunity for the realization and recognition of these feelings and attitudes. Because they belong to the whole conference, the appropriate setting is a plenary session. But because they are looking backwards and inwards to the conference, they are put near, but not at, the end. They are not intended to provide closure, but only to prepare for ending.

Any attempt to suggest that conferences of this kind can be summed up in a few words would be a denial of the experience that members have been through. The task of the plenary reviews is to try to help members to end the conference but not to stop learning. In the process they might be able to crystallize some aspects of the totality of their experience.

A number of ways of staging and conducting plenary reviews have been tried. The initiative has been left to members, with the chairman or programme director acting as seminar leader; or one or more members of the staff have taken the initiative by giving a review. Members and staff have been mixed together in the audience; or some staff have been on the platform, with others grouped at the back of the room or to one side.

To leave the initiative entirely with members implies a number of unproven assumptions: that member-staff relations have reached such a point of resolution that members can and will express their views publicly; that members have learnt sufficient to be able to articulate their views coherently; that they have had enough time to prepare for the sessions to make them effective; and that the staff have no further contribution to make except in general discussion. I prefer staff initiative – at least to the extent of setting the scene. This assumes that the staff still have some contribution to make to the learning process. For the same reason, I also prefer to stage the reviews with the total staff on the platform. On occasions when hostility towards the staff has not been fully worked out, this can be and has been interpreted as aggressive and threatening; but I think it is preferable to mixing staff and members, or to having staff at the side or back of the room. At least with staff on the platform members know at whom they are shooting and whence the staff fire will come. Putting the whole staff on the platform also gives a visual demonstration of their collective responsibility for the conference. No arrangement of seating can stop those in the front rows from feeling that they are being shot in the back by other members sitting behind them; but this phenomenon has at least been explored in the large-group sessions.

There are two review sessions. Until recent conferences, into which we have introduced the large-group event, I had started the first session by giving an account of what I had observed of the conference in my role as conference director. I had tried to state what my experience had been, and what I believed I had learnt from it. I did not try to tell members what I thought they should have learnt, but, by talking about what I thought I had learnt, I tried to set a framework for a discussion in which others, members and staff, could give their versions of their experience. My hope was that, by making the statement personal, I would encourage others to make a personal assessment as well. This behaviour has seemed to me to be consistent with my role as director. The point of view was unique, and was the only one that was consistently concerned with the total conference.

Some of the results of this approach have been described in Chapter 6. It was the experience of unsatisfactory reviews that led to the introduction of the large-group event. Once that event had been introduced we had to rethink our methods of dealing with the review. One conclusion about previous reviews was that, by doing as elaborate a job as I had done, I had made it difficult for the staff, let alone the members, to introduce different frameworks or even to put forward constructive alternative explanations within the framework I had given. I had thus made it difficult for other individual contributions to be much more than destructive criticism. By exercising my authority I had also given a demonstration of power that made it impossible at that stage of the conference for the members to combine effectively to oppose me. I had reasserted my leadership and thus, far from preparing to end the conference, I had gone back to the beginning and restarted it. The complaints that I had 'blinded the members with science' had much reality, and they were right to be resentful when, having raised expectations of a lecturer-audience relationship by my opening, I had subsequently answered questions with interpretations of their behaviour.

As a result of thinking about the changes required, we have now modified the presentation of the opening. In it I define the task of the review as a continuation of the conference process, as a further opportunity to learn about interpersonal and intergroup relations and particularly to learn about their ending. I draw attention to any particularly significant events and then leave it to members to take up what they wish. I do not think we have yet got this event right, probably because we are too aware of the pitfalls involved. On the one hand there is little we can teach; on the other we must not concentrate so much on our own problems that we either ignore those of the members or, worse, claim their sympathy for our difficulties.

This opening, which takes only five to ten minutes, is usually followed by questions about conference design and about the differences between training and therapy, all of which the members of the staff try to answer as fully as they can. At one conference there was criticism in the first review session of the timing and the content of some events, but the staff came away feeling that it had been a profitable session. The second session, later on the same day, was very different. It opened by a member's saying that he dreaded it, but he did not explain why. There were long periods of silence, and the silences were tense. I was told that I had evaded every question I had been asked in the first session, but little evidence was produced to support this view. It is true that to a large number of the questions that had been asked we had not given satisfactory answers; and what members found difficult to tolerate was that we really had no satisfactory answers to give. And the discussion veered onto the topic of how you became better at our job.

'How do you become a big cheese in this field?'

'Big cheeses take a long time to mature.'

Nobody added, and I regret I did not think of it myself at the time, that big, mature, cheeses can also smell.

Members discussed ending, and the inappropriateness of exchanging ritual compliments in such a conference. Between contributions there were longer and longer silences. After some time, I began to feel that a new ritual had been invented – sitting out time. There had been some comments on the remarkably good time-keeping at the conference, and as I thought about them I realized that a decision had been taken by the members: to sit out the session but to do no more work. Unfortunately, it took me a long time to work out that this was what was happening, and to review the data that supported my conclusion. Eventually, some minutes before the end of the session I became convinced that my observation was correct and so I made it to the members. I suggested that this ritual, like others, was being used to deny the need to work, but I added that it was now so late in the review that the work would have to be left for the application groups. I then closed the session ahead of time.

At other conferences I have not felt such an abandonment of the task and the session has ended like others, on time, but with no conclusions reached. Though it is difficult to relate cause and effect, it is noticeable that reviews conducted in this way are invariably followed by very hard-working application groups. In this sense they may be achieving their purpose of ending the conference without applying closure to learning.

PART III

The Conference Institution

CHAPTER 10

The Life of the Conference

Explorations in Group Relations (Trist and Sofer, 1959) described how members came to accept the different roles taken by staff and developed their own 'member' culture. The institution of the 'night shift' dealt with many of the stresses and strains felt by various members, and provided a mechanism by which members could help each other. Today, after many more conferences have been held, there appears to be less improvisation by the members and hence less building of a member culture that is different from the general culture of the conference.

Members still sit up late at night to discuss what is going on in the conference; they still spend much of their spare time criticizing conference methods and comparing staff performances; also, they still have to deal with stress and strain, which for some members often become acute. But they sit up late to discuss other things as well. So far as I am aware, there has never again been a 'permanent night shift', which was such a remarkable feature of the first conference. Nor have members developed since that conference such a special semi-derisory jargon of their own – *Grüppenfuhrer* for group consultants, for example – as a means of testing out ideas while limiting their investment in them. The jargon that becomes common currency tends to be the jargon of the conference, the concepts used are those promulgated in the lectures and other events.

I can only observe that the atmosphere outside the actual events appears to have become less generally tense than it was in that first conference. There are, I believe, a number of reasons for these changes, some of which I propose to discuss in this chapter. But the overriding reason is undoubtedly that for both members and staff the conferences are no longer a 'first' experience, even though, for many, their previous experience has not been direct. Not only the uncertainty of outcome but the excitement of a 'first' has inevitably diminished.

MEMBER-STAFF RELATIONS

As the staff have gained experience in the roles expected of them and have felt therefore a greater security in taking them, they have set a surer pattern of behaviour. This has communicated itself to members and has thus affected the climate of the whole conference. It allows members to accept the staff in their various roles and, perhaps, to be less critical of lapses from them. Members have less expectation of staff omnipotence and omniscience, or less need to test their pretence. Even though every conference is different, the fact that they have experienced so many conferences has been a major source of learning for the staff. Although they cannot make specific predictions they now know the kinds of feeling and attitude they will have to cope with; they know far more what they can and what they cannot deal with.

A symptom of this increased confidence is the staff attitude to members who leave during the conference. With uncertainty about conference aims and methods, any threat to leave part-way through, any sign of unbearable strain in a member, invariably led to so much anxiety in the staff group that whoever was threatening to leave occupied almost their whole attention. This in its turn tended to magnify the symptoms of strain. The member concerned became, in effect, the 'leader' of the conference. Anything that happened was first examined in relation to his going or staying, and decisions were often taken, not in the interests of the conference as a whole, but in the interests of avoiding his departure. Departure was in itself implicitly assumed to be a sign of conference failure.

Today, the clearer definition of the conference task, and the firmer conference structure, make it easier to decide what belongs in the conference and what does not. Those who wish to leave, leave. I do not want to imply that neither the staff nor myself worry about incidents of this kind; we do, but I do not believe we now sacrifice other members' interests to our worry, or so absorb it into the staff group that conference management becomes paralysed. We hope that, before a member leaves, he will feel that there are adequate formal mechanisms available through which he can get any advice he needs, or at least discuss his leaving, whatever the reasons.

Just as I do not wish to imply that the staff no longer worry about early departures, neither do I wish to imply that the firmer drawing of conference boundaries and the firmer control of internal communication systems have dealt with the problem of members' reliance on each other during periods of stress. In the first conference we introduced a tutorial system to try to take some of the burden from the members. It was hardly used, members apparently preferring their own institution. One criticism was that the tutorial system was a 'built-in' invitation to members to make individual relationships with particular staff members, and these cut across every other established relationship in the conference. Given the choice, members' loyalty to each other, and to the staff members conducting the various conference events, was stronger than individual need for a personal tutorial relationship. If by chance any of the tutors were also study- or application-group leaders, the conflict of loyalties was exacerbated. Still more, if any of the tutors were also, outside the conference, psychiatrists or psychotherapists, the 'built-in' invitation was therapeutically oriented, an orientation which was inappropriate in an educational institution.[1]

One danger of the strengthening of conference boundaries and control systems is that members might feel less responsible than they did formerly for those of their own number who are suffering considerable stress. They can assume that the 'management' has accepted full responsibility, and hence can feel free to project their own stress onto the potential casualty. They can also feel that they need do nothing about the consequences of their projection, except perhaps vent their fury on a potential casualty who refuses to remain one. This, as has been discussed in the chapter on the large-group event, is an evasion of a normal human responsibility for the consequences of one's own behaviour. While a catastrophe may provide a remarkable learning opportunity, its occurrence does not necessarily help the casualty who provides it, nor does it help members to face their own guilt about their contribution to it. It is important that neither members nor staff – and since staff are responsible for the total conference, particularly the staff – should overestimate the efficiency of the control systems now established.

In practice, the staff are now generally able to behave more spontaneously than they could in the earlier conferences. Whether or not they visit the bar, common to both members and staff, is left much more to individual feeling. Where they sit at meals is more a matter of personal choice. In the early conferences, staff felt that it was their duty to visit the bar when members would be present, and that as a matter of policy they should not sit together in a staff huddle at meals. Self-consciously, they mixed with members. Today, if individual staff feel that they do not want to go into the bar, they do not do so. If they want to sit together at meals,

1 The difference between an educational institution and a clinical institution is discussed more fully in Chapter 12.

they sit together. Where they drink and where they eat have still, of course, some meaning in the development of the conference culture; but now that these are matters of personal choice rather than of deliberately planned policy, their behaviour can become a less biased subject for examination and hence contribute more to conference learning.

Perhaps more importantly, if staff behave in ways they feel to be right at the time, by implication they free members to do likewise, and so total conference behaviour becomes more spontaneous and as a learning experience more fruitful. Not only do members feel free to exclude staff from their discussions at the bar and at meals; but they also feel less inhibited about approaching staff members with their questions when they want to.

Experience shows that, in the early part of a conference, there is a tendency for both staff and members to want to remain segregated; for staff to stick to their own common room and stay together at meals. During the middle of the conference it is noticeable that staff and members mix together more freely. Towards the end of the conference, there is again a tendency to separate. The staff pull back because they are becoming preoccupied with conference progress and what more they should do, if anything, about the imminent end. Members are preoccupied with the end of the conference, and what they have or have not got from it; the dying hope that the staff have all, or most of, the answers makes them want to stand back to make their own re-evaluation of the experience.

FORMAL AND INFORMAL CHANNELS OF COMMUNICATION

It is a great temptation for the staff to use every means possible to find out what is happening in the conference: how members are feeling about their experiences, and what they are learning, if anything. The staff are always anxious about the impact of the conference on the members and the extent to which they are being disturbed by the conference events. Casual social contact at the bar, at meals, or at coffee- and tea-breaks provides ample opportunities for the informal exchange of information. Direct questions about why some events are conducted as they are or why staff are behaving in a particular manner are always referred to the appropriate event or the appropriate staff member.

In principle, informal channels of communication can be no substitute for the formal communication system. In other institutions, informal channels are frequently more important than formal ones, and are used to bolster ineffective systems. Examination of this phenomenon is pertinent to the conference task. Staff therefore try to avoid, as far as possible, going into collusion with the grapevine system of communication in the conference. If the staff in general, and the director in particular, are not getting adequate information through conference events and the normal administrative machinery, then this is regarded as a symptom that something is wrong with the formal communication system. To obtain information informally, and to be inhibited by the setting in which it is obtained from taking appropriate action, deny the possibility of using the information for learning.

My own experience of organizations is that frequently both the formal and the informal channels of communication are so well recognized and accepted that questions that should be asked about weaknesses in the formal system are obscured by the excellence of the informal one. In the same way, the presence in an organization of individuals who are adept at getting things done in spite of the rules and procedures laid down, frequently obscures, or at least avoids action about, organizational weakness. In the conferences, formal channels that are blocked to the extent that informal channels have to be used, and organizational weaknesses that have to be overcome by gifted individuals, are precisely what should be examined. Blocked communications and organizational weakness are seldom due only to the incompetence of their designers; they are invariably motivated. One task of the conference is to expose the motivations, and to rehearse other means than bypassing to deal with blocks in communications, and other means than the appointment of superfluous co-ordinators and liaison officers to deal with organizational weakness.

The communications sent to members before the conference starts are as factual as we can make them; we make no attempt to state theory or to describe what might happen. In addition to being told the location of the conference, the time of starting, convenient trains, and the conference telephone number, members are informed in what study and application groups they will be; who will be their consultants; who will be the other members of their groups; and even in which rooms the groups will meet. Though some of this information may be meaningless – in the sense that members usually have no acquaintance with the building in which the conference is to be held or with the staff – we have found that such attention to detail does reassure some members, if only about the administrative competence of conference management.

Before they arrive members have filled in two forms: one booking a place at the conference and giving basic personal information; the second giving some details of their background and experience. These forms are used to allocate members to study and application groups. On the information available, mistakes can be, and are, made. Some prospective members know each other personally, though from their addresses, occupations, and interests this is not discernible; some may be superior and subordinate in the same organization, a fact that is obscured by the retention of original company names after a successful take-over bid. In the information sent out, members are asked to let us know about any mistakes of this kind so that we can correct them.

The giving of this preliminary information not only cuts down what has to be told to members about the domestic and administrative arrangements when they arrive, but also sets the pattern for the conference itself. The staff hope to demonstrate their competence but not their omniscience.

As has been mentioned earlier, no name labels are issued. Apart from the difficulty of finding labels that are large enough for the shortsighted to read without glasses and at the same time small enough not to be an intrusion, labels are a conventional way of avoiding the problems of finding out who and what people are. It is in keeping with this policy, too, that the tone of the opening plenary, which has already been described, is set. The intention is to make it a factual statement of events and their purpose, with the minimum of prediction about how members are likely to feel or what is likely to happen.

Such communications and such behaviour represent the first steps in removing some of the conventional trappings that are used to obscure the processes of group formation, and in lowering some of the conventional defences that are used to avoid problems of interpersonal and intergroup relations.

It is noticeable that in the interval between the opening plenary session and the first study group, usually a tea interval, the noise of conversation between members is loud. Sometimes members have asked:

'How do you achieve such a remarkable get-together in so short a time?'

'You just give us a list of members' names, but you don't identify anybody but the staff, and here we are, half an hour later, talking as though we had known each other for years.'

'I suppose letting us get on with it ourselves is a part of the technique.'

In one sense, yes. When the normal props of introduction and labels are removed, members do take an increased responsibility for introducing themselves and for getting to know one another. It is also possible, however, that the removal of some conventional defences right at the beginning leads members to erect others, and that one of them is a determination not to be anxious, or to show it. Members display a determined – perhaps overdetermined – intention to demonstrate 'togetherness', as a means of avoiding the anticipated possibility of conflict and separateness.

MANAGEMENT–MEMBER RELATIONSHIPS

For the same reason, the management does not initiate the organization of any members' committees, or any kind of joint consultative activities between members and itself. The conference is about leadership, and this involves the interpersonal and intergroup relations between members, between members and staff, and between 'management' as represented by the director and secretary and both members and staff. The relations between director and staff will be discussed in the next chapter. Here I am concerned with members and the management they face in the actual conference.

A management initiative to set up consultative machinery would convey the unmistakable message that the staff regarded joint consultation as a procedure whose usefulness for·the solving of problems of interpersonal and intergroup relations need not be questioned. It may be a possible solution to some of them, but the method of setting it up, the overt reason for it, and the motives behind it are all problems the conference exists to study. Staff initiative to design and set up a consultative procedure might thus avoid examination of what often lies underneath many of the overt problems of relationship between leaders and followers. The majority of members who come to these conferences are well experienced, if not in setting up joint consultative procedures, at least in working with them. There is, of course, nothing in the conference structure to stop members taking some initiative, or using conference events for this purpose. The important thing is that such initiative, or lack of it, should be studied. In particular, the intergroup exercise provides opportunities for the study of the reasons and motives for many of the difficulties that are frequently hidden or at least evaded by methods of election, procedures at meetings, and the like.

The very creation of joint consultative machinery, with the appointment of representatives of predetermined groups or more usually of categories of members, is often unconsciously designed to obscure the possibility that loyalties may be more divided than it is convenient to examine, and that some bonds across the lines of demarcation would, if given the chance, be stronger than those that have been predetermined. In the conference there are the staff who have organized it and the members who come to it. If the intergroup exercise – which has not yet happened – did lead to the formation of a committee of members to meet the 'management', then that would be an outcome of a conference event and could be used for further learning.

I should add that, from the point of view of learning about intergroup relations, it would probably be better if conference management as represented by the staff group were not a part of the intergroup exercise. Consultants to groups or to intergroup meetings could then concentrate only on the underlying processes of relationships between groups of members and avoid the complication of the imposed conference authority. The complexities of the relationships between conference management and exercise direction, in which the same members of the staff group take roles as consultants to members and as members of management, would not arise. But this change would require some other event, and time for it, that would provide members with the opportunity to use their learning about intergroup relations to work out their management-member relationships.

In any organized activity, the members of a management group have to accept collective responsibility for overall management. If they also take operational or specialist roles, they always have to face a possible conflict between their share of responsibility for overall management and their responsibility for their own individual activities. In the conferences members inevitably attempt to deal with their hostility to authority by trying to separate their consultants from management. The director, as the symbol of management, is an obvious target for hostility and he has to be able to tolerate the hatred involved. But both members and staff have to come to terms with the staff's share in his appointment. At present the opportunity for the exploration of these problems is found in the intergroup exercise; with a modified exercise that excluded management as a group, some other opportunity would have to be found. Management-member relations would then fall properly into the application phase. This modification will, I believe, be possible only in an institution that lasts longer than the present conferences. Already we feel that each series of events is very short, and to add a new kind of application phase would make them shorter still.[1]

The conference programme is the best that the staff can devise in the light of their experience of conferences of this kind. They take account of the amount and intensity of the work to be done, and of the need for time to relax and recuperate between events. It would, however, be playing to the omniscient fantasies of both members and staff to imagine that staff can predict always just when rest is needed and just when events should be timed to start and finish. Since the programme is printed months in advance of the conference, other events can intervene, and chance can play its part in making some of the timings unsuitable. For example, because of changes of staff for unavoidable reasons after the programme has been issued, it may be impossible to run some events, either at the time scheduled or at all. Members, too, may have real needs for change that could not have been foreseen when the programme was being compiled.

The important point is that once a programme has been decided, it should be adhered to if possible, and requests for changes should be scrutinized to ascertain as far as possible the reality of the need for them. Since it is the programme that, in the first place, governs management-member relationships, changes may often be suggested in an attempt to embarrass or express hostility to management. Changes can be made if reality demands them, but management has to be aware that requests for change can also be used by members, or even by staff, to manipulate relationships in the conference itself.

So far, our experience in the new series of conferences has been that requests for change are rare. In other words, members sense the reality behind the programme and, though they may have doubts about some of it, they nevertheless accept that experience alone will show how right or wrong the timing has been.

The conferences are designed to provide a continuous check on reality. The methods used challenge preconceived attitudes and beliefs – the stereotypes on which so many interpersonal and intergroup relations are based. They question existing value systems and the basis of human beliefs. The preoccupations of members and staff alike are with the new challenge to their understanding of each other and of themselves. It is rare for members to say they have enjoyed a conference. It is common for them to be grateful for the experience.

[1] Nevertheless, in June 1965 a two-part intergroup exercise, the first without a management group, the second with, will be tried.

CHAPTER 11

The Staff Group

In the 1957 conference, conference management was, as now, in the hands of the staff group. The 'officers' were a chairman of an executive committee, representing the two sponsoring organizations; a programme director; and two joint secretaries, one drawn from each of the organizing bodies. At the conference the chairman of the executive committee acted as chairman of all plenary sessions and as chairman of the staff group at staff meetings. The programme director's task was to coordinate conference plans, and to take technical leadership in staff meetings about the programme, both before it started and while it was being implemented. Neither took part in any of the small-group events.

In practice, the chairman took the lead in administrative affairs, with responsibility for conference arrangements, and the programme director took the lead in technical and professional matters. The joint conference secretaries had much the same task as the secretary has now: to supervise administration, to implement policy so far as it affects the domestic arrangements, to run the conference office, and to help members as far as she can. Through her is manifested much of the staff group's concern for individuals and their welfare. The chairman acted, and was treated, as a chairman, and the programme director as an adviser. Neither was vested with executive authority, which remained with the staff group collectively.

By the nature of the roles they take in a conference, consultants have to work on their own. Theirs is a professional task. When they are acting in study groups, in groups of the intergroup exercise, or in application groups, they have to take full responsibility for what happens. Decisions about whether to intervene, how to intervene, and how to behave, are theirs and theirs only. They have to be given and to accept the corresponding authority. Hence, neither the staff group nor its officers can determine what happens in events that are conducted by consultants. A programme director can advise, condole, or even try to bully, but in the event what the consultant does is up to him. However loyal consultants may feel to the staff group and to its officers, and however conscientiously they may try to follow a programme director's advice, they must be governed by what they believe to be happening to the group for which, at the time, they are responsible. If there is a conflict of opinion and they have to choose between a programme director's policy and what they themselves feel to be right, they have to discard the director's policy. In professional work it is no alibi, when something goes wrong, to claim that it went wrong because the consultant was doing what he was told to do.

In starting any new kind of multidisciplinary programme differences of opinion among the staff are inevitable. From the early conferences onwards the staff have come from a variety of backgrounds and experiences and have been trained in different disciplines. There are those whose experience is mainly in psychiatric or psycho-analytic practice, some of whom have had experience of taking therapeutic groups; there are others whose more important experiences have been with problems of organization, whose disciplines are psychology, sociology, or anthropology, and whose group experience was in the early Tavistock training groups. More recently, as will be described in Chapter 13, members of staff have included some whose group experience has been in these conferences and whose disciplines have not been in the social sciences. At first there could not be, and there still is not, any generally agreed technique for the conduct of particular events or of the conference as a whole. Though with longer experience of working together there is more agreement than there was, the agreement is general rather than particular. But whatever the level of agreement or disagreement, a programme director cannot direct events in which he is not working as a consultant.

At the same time, a chairman who is not technically responsible for the programme can have little or no professional authority in the staff group. We had made the assumption that the staff would have agreed on a general policy and on the programme before the conference started. They had; but what had not been foreseen was that agreement on policy and programme had implied, in all our minds, agreement on the conduct of events within the programme. Because of our different backgrounds and different training we approached our tasks in groups differently; and in discussions after the sessions we took a long time to appreciate our underlying similarities. In the process we made life very difficult for our officers. The situation was also complicated by our holding the conferences in buildings that were under the control of other institutions and, however obliging the owners, we had to conform to their regulations.

More importantly, we had assumed that if, in a conference, decisions had to be taken about whether to change the programme, how to conduct some particular public event, how to improvise on the use of available accommodation, or how to interpret what was happening, the chairman would call a staff meeting and the meeting would decide. Our earlier differences continued into these meetings. It became clear that in a fortnight's conference of intensive work events moved too quickly for such 'work-through' processes to be effective unless they were based on a far more detailed policy agreed beforehand. Moreover, since most of the public events, except the lectures, were conducted by the chairman and programme director, theirs were the only spontaneous performances that came under staff-group scrutiny and hence criticism. They had to carry heavy responsibilities on behalf of the staff, but had little or no collective sanction from the staff for what they did.

In conferences of this kind, the better consultants do their jobs in their own events, the more are they likely to become absorbed by their jobs and by those events. In the intergroup exercise a consultant to a group struggles with his own group's problems in relation to other groups, in a study group he is occupied with what is going on inside that group, and in an application group he is working hard to understand applications in a new field of work. He is concerned with the effect of other events of the conference on the group for which he is responsible, but his concern is with the ways in which his own group is helped or hindered, not with the other events as such. The very nature of the consultant's responsibilities determines his major preoccupations. To some extent what he is doing is what matters. And, indeed, it is right that consultants should take this view. They have their responsibilities, and must have the necessary authority to discharge them. If they feel that what is happening elsewhere in the conference is having a damaging effect on the task they are trying to perform, they must want changes to allow them to improve that performance. As members of the staff group they have to accept a collective responsibility for the whole conference, but the more they become absorbed in their own specialist roles, the more they regard the conference from the specialist's point of view.

REORGANIZATION OF CONFERENCE MANAGEMENT

These early experiences led us, in preparation for the 1962 conference, to re-examine staff roles generally, and in particular those of chairman and programme director. In between 1957 and 1962 there had been some modifications in these roles. In 1959 and 1960 both chairman and programme director had taken part in small-group events. After the 1960 conference the effect of this change received considerable attention and a lot of time was spent in trying to thrash out some of the problems of technique. As a result, in the 1961 conference, though the chairman continued active in some group events, the programme director was once more pulled out of them. His only active role, *vis-à-vis* the members, was in plenary sessions. The need for some officer of the staff group to be free to take an overall view of what was happening in the conference without immersion in small-group activities had been reaffirmed.

In our review of the 1961 conference in preparation for 1962, we recognized that while we had again withdrawn the programme director from specific events to enable him to take an overall view we had given him no authority to do anything about the view he had thereby obtained. He had never had any executive power and, by excluding him once more from what were felt by other members of the staff group to be important events in the conference, we had succeeded in emasculating him again.

When we looked at what we had expected of the chairman, we found that we had demanded the impossible. His job had been to try to maintain some kind of order at staff meetings, to try to get the meetings to arrive at decisions when no real consensus could be reached. In consequence, staff meetings had become almost endless, both before and during the conference, and yet, in spite of this, some important decisions had gone by default. Indecision in conference management had been communicated to members in many different ways but seldom in ways that made it possible for members to use the learning opportunities thus provided. For the most part, staff difficulties in reaching decisions had aroused members' sympathies and had not led to critical examination. Furthermore, they involved the staff in long and exhausting meetings at times when they too needed to rest. This had led to such frustration among the staff that subgroups had tended to form round opposing views and their sponsors, with the inevitable exacerbation of management difficulties.

The need for a relatively detached overall view of the conference, as it proceeded, was once more reaffirmed. It was also accepted, however, that decisions had to be made at the conference itself – and before it for that matter – that would not necessarily meet with the unqualified approval of all the staff. We had to accept that we could no longer go on

147

behaving as if group leadership was the only kind of executive leadership available. We felt that if differences of opinion arose after overall policy had been agreed, authority for its interpretation and implementation had to be delegated; and that this authority had to be delegated by the staff group to the conference officers. We had avoided this problem previously by naming two officers, and giving neither sufficient executive authority.

We decided that the roles of chairman and programme director should be combined into one role – that of conference director. The conference director would be given responsibility for the overall conduct of the conference, and authority to make any decisions that he felt to be necessary to discharge that responsibility. We examined which decisions he could take and which he could not take: he could not take decisions about a consultant's method of intervention or behaviour in the events for which the consultant was responsible, but he could take decisions about the programme, about the staff roles in plenary sessions, and about staff responsibility for other than programmed activities. Some of the consequences of this clarification have been described in the chapters on conference structure and culture. We like to feel that our own conference learning, though slow, has ultimately been profitable.

THE DIRECTOR'S ROLE IN PRACTICE

This is the role I was given by the staff for the 1962 conference and which I have taken in subsequent Leicester/Tavistock conferences and others. It is the role from which I am writing this account. At the beginning I did not want it. Nevertheless, I have found the experience rewarding and have become fascinated, in consequence, by the problems of building and maintaining a new type of educational institution. I shall discuss some of these in the chapter on institutional reproduction.

I could not have taken the role as we designed it had I not taken it with the full sanction of the rest of the conference staff. Nor would the office have been tenable without their continued support. There have been many disagreements on both technical and practical grounds, both before and during conferences. But I have been permitted to exercise the authority vested in me. When in a staff meeting we have failed to reach a consensus of opinion, I have been able to announce a decision and, even though it has run contrary to the views of some of the staff who have been bound by it, I have known that, in practice, the decision will be implemented. Moreover, I have also known that subsequent discussion of the effect of the decision will be reasonably objective, and not too impossibly coloured by any disagreement that has preceded it.

By nature of the role I fill and the tasks I actually perform in the conference, I see far more of the staff than I do of the members, and I see the staff for the most part only when they are off duty. Apart from social occasions, my contacts with members are generally collective. I meet them only in open plenary sessions, sometimes as consultant to the large group, or as director of the intergroup exercise. I experience their feelings and attitudes directly only when they are expressed publicly or socially. I do not meet the small face-to-face groups in which I could experience for myself the reality of their more intimate relationships with each other and with me. My small-group contacts are with staff, all of whom, except the secretary, are closely identified with the small groups within the conference.

I have found the role of director a lonely one. My colleagues always appear to be doing the exciting things, having the revealing experiences, bringing about the changes in members' attitudes. All I can feel that I have done is to provide a framework in which these things can happen. And a framework is cold and uncomfortable when others are having the close personal contacts with the members for whom the conference is designed. In the staff common room, after almost any small-group event, consultants are full of their experiences, experiences that I wish I had had.

This has been driven home to me recently in our experiments with shorter conferences. In collaboration with Christian Teamwork, we have run both four-day and six-day conferences. In the four-day conference, we simply could not afford to have the number of staff that would have been required to permit the director to be left out of small-group activities. Therefore, in addition to taking the role of director, which involved responsibility for conference opening and review, I gave a lecture, and acted as consultant to a study group and an application group. I had little view of the conference as a whole. Part of the trouble was that in so short a conference we were under terrific pressure and had inadequate time for staff meetings, but the major difficulty was that I was so involved with the small groups for which I was responsible that I had too little attention to spare for my colleagues' struggles. For long periods each day I found it difficult even to be interested in what they were doing and what results they were getting. In the six-day conference I have reverted to the role of conference director and have taken no part in study groups.

In staff meetings, members of the staff, of course, speak from their own experiences. When I try to fit their views into an overall view of the total conference process, I am often seen as, and I feel myself, out of tune with one or more of them, particularly when their experiences do not appear to have been the same; or when, as frequently happens, experience in one kind of event appears to contradict experience in another kind. In this situation my observations of staff relations, my feelings about them and my sense of their feelings about me, are the only evidence I have for what is really happening. I have already discussed, for example, in the chapter on the intergroup exercise, my sense that relations between member groups are projected directly into the staff common room. When the staff start criticizing my direction of the exercise, I can infer that the members want to quarrel with me also, and that they have succeeded in getting the staff to take up the cudgels on their behalf. Their criticisms may be valid, and I may have to change my mind; but if the members' object has been to split the staff and they look like succeeding, I have to take account of that as well, and in the light of it make judgements about the validity of the criticism.

STAFF RELATIONSHIPS

What has to be remembered at all times – and it is the director's job to remember it – is that the conference is about leadership and management, not only of small and large groups but of institutions as well. The objects of study are the interpersonal and intergroup relations involved in those functions, and the staff themselves are a group that has an appointed leader. The leadership of the staff group and the management of the conference are, therefore, subjects for study at the conference. Staff interpersonal and intergroup relations are part of the life of the conference itself. If the staff cannot learn from experience of their own interpersonal and intergroup relationships, then it is unlikely that they will be able to help the members to learn from theirs. The same point is made by Fichelet, Meignier, Michelat, and Yaun (1963):

'But it seems that the possibility of projection and the analysis of projection require a certain type of relationship among the analysts themselves. In the first place this relationship must be based on an analysis by the analysts themselves of their own inter-personal and group relations (otherwise, they would unconsciously provide the members with a model that would forbid analysis of inter-personal or group relations between themselves or with the analysts).'

When, as happens, a disagreement occurs between two members of the staff about what should be done – and, be it said, the disagreements are usually between one or other of my colleagues and myself – apart from dealing with the subject of the dispute, we also have to ask why this particular quarrel is taking place, at this time, and why between these two. What are the dynamics of the staff group itself which is precipitating it? How far is it a group process in which the group is displacing its anxiety about the conference as a whole or an event in it onto two members who are expressing the conflict on its behalf? How far do we believe in the new messianic leader to be produced by the pair?

When I am involved I have to ask whether my own anxiety about my performance is making me even more obstinate than usual. How far is the difficulty due to my capacity for blackmailing my colleagues by threats to resign the role of director? How far am I using the authority delegated to me in an inappropriate way? How far is the quarrel due to the intransigence of the colleagues with whom I am in dispute? Is the disagreement based on genuine technical differences or does it arise mainly from different views of the conference and its events? These questions are not peculiar to conference direction, they are inherent in any discussion about policy in any group that is responsible for leading and managing. What is important for a staff group running a conference that is itself about leadership and management is that the group's attention to its own difficulties should sufficiently differentiate fantasy and reality for the result, as it affects the members, to enhance learning opportunities.

One of the difficulties of separating reality from fantasy is the toleration of uncertainty of outcome demanded of the staff. In a staff meeting, anyone who expresses a point of view with sufficient strength, or seems sure in his prediction, tends to wield more influence than either the point of view or the prediction sometimes deserves. One consequence is that when I exercise decisively the authority delegated to me, I can sometimes do so with more power than I was intended to have. The very demonstration of power makes it more difficult for others effectively to oppose the decision. In addition, because of the need to make drastic economies in the time (and money) spent in pre-conference planning, almost all administrative decisions have been left to the conference secretary and myself. But 'administrative' decisions, particularly those that have to do with what is sent out to inquirers and to members, are frequently found, like administrative decisions elsewhere, to have modified or even predetermined the policy they were intended only to implement. In solving some problems we have now to beware that our solutions do not serve to suppress other problems that need equal attention.

Nevertheless, the acceptance of the difficulties that arise has exercised a useful discipline on us. We have disagreed, but we have avoided some of the disagreements that would have arisen, not from real differences of opinion, but from our anxiety about the new events that we were attempting. We have been forced to pay attention to the role of director and to his relationships with the staff group, and to examine the trust that members of the staff are prepared to place in each other's competence. Unlimited time to work out our differences could have led, and could still lead, to inaction, and to the destruction of any leadership.

The real testing time for staff relationships is towards the end of the conference. The staff experience many of the same emotions as the members. They too are depressed by the ending of events, are aware of the missed opportunities and the waste of time; they too wish they could start some things over again. Even though they hope to have other opportunities in other conferences, that is small consolation for the ending of the current one. The difficulties intensify as the conference review sessions approach. Application groups are experiencing the flatness that follows the ending of the 'here and now' events, and the depression of realizing that while conference learning may have helped towards a wider understanding of many problems in human relations, it has not provided any magical solutions. In this sense the conference review sessions provide a last chance to produce a dramatic result, or, at least, to pull everything neatly together. The temptation to forget lost opportunities in earlier parts of the conference by getting false closure at the end makes accurate judgement about the best way to conduct reviews almost impossible.

Discussion about what is to be said in opening the review, and how the rest is to be conducted, reveals the different points of view among the staff. Since I am the only member of the staff group who has not been involved in small groups, I tend to feel that I know most about the conference as a whole; my colleagues, who have been in intimate touch with members in small-group activities, feel, and rightly so, that they know more about the feelings and attitudes of individuals. In consequence, they often find me too preoccupied with the structure and culture of the conference; I, in my turn, often find them too preoccupied with personalities and small-group relations. But all of us are having to cope with our own mixed feelings about ending. In spite of our experience of many conferences, we cannot help hoping that this time we shall pull off something spectacular. We also know that if we did it would be a fantasy.

CHAPTER 12

Training or Therapy

The conferences I have been trying to describe represent one application of an understanding of human relationships that has developed in the Tavistock Clinic and Institute and elsewhere over many years. The group of psychiatrists and psychologists who formed the original staff of the Institute had been brought together in the British Army during the Second World War. Many psychiatrists and psychologists in the army found themselves dealing more with social than with individual problems, and of necessity recruited other social scientists to extend their understanding of institutions and their organizations. They became concerned with the health of groups, both small and large, as well as with that of individuals. They found themselves increasingly focusing attention on the relationships within and between groups, that were the accompaniment, if not the cause, of individual breakdown.

In the immediate postwar period the use of groups for psychotherapy was stimulated by the need to make psychiatric and psychological help available to more and more individuals. Individual treatment would have required an impractical and impossible increase in cost, even if there had been enough psychotherapists to give it. But the use of groups for the treatment of individual disorders in turn stimulated thinking and research about the disorders themselves. In this new thinking the individual was looked upon not only as a person suffering from some particular disease but also as the focus of a disturbed relationship network, as a role carrier on behalf of others. His disorder was seen, in part at least, as the result of a complex interaction process. The study of patient groups has led to more understanding of individual as well as of group psychology.

At the same time, the understanding of groups that had developed from work in the wartime army was used by the newly independent Tavistock Institute, not only in its research and consulting work but also for the training of its staff and students. There are now many different approaches to 'group' work. At this early stage of our understanding of human relationships and our knowledge of techniques for studying them, I believe it important that a variety of approaches and techniques should develop both independently and interdependently. It would be fatal if we spent too much time in a premature attempt to find a single unified approach to either therapy or training.

In group therapy there are two kinds of technical approach – or perhaps it would be better to say one approach with two polarities. At the one, attention is focused on the individual's relations with the group, the group is the background against which individual behaviour is examined; at the other, attention is focused on the group as a group, individual behaviour is seen not as a part of individual psychological make-up, but as a manifestation of a group process. The use of groups as a means of providing opportunities to learn about interpersonal and intergroup relations derives from the latter approach.

In discussions at and about conferences we are often asked to explain the difference between training and therapy and to discriminate between the techniques used. Training and therapy are both concerned with change; training in human relations and psychotherapy are both concerned with increasing an understanding of the motives for, and causes of, human behaviour. In this sense they are at different points on a continuum. If one purpose of education is defined as the provision of opportunities for maturation and growth, then the aim of psychotherapy could be defined as the removal of some of the barriers to accepting the opportunities.

The confusion, to my mind, as far as the purpose of conferences is in question, arises largely from the similarity between study and therapeutic groups in respect of their size and the techniques used, without adequate reference being made to the institutions in which the groups are held. The confusion has not been helped by the fact that we use consultants who are responsible for therapy groups in the Tavistock Clinic as consultants to conference groups of various kinds. Their techniques of 'taking' groups, since in both settings they are trying to understand what is happening in the 'here and now' of the group, are inevitably similar. And since much of what happens in any group – study or therapy – whose task is to examine its own behaviour is the same, the consultants' interventions not only point to the same kind of phenomena but are often couched in the same kind of language. These similarities have helped to obscure the responsibility the consultant carries, the authority he exercises, and the sanctions under which he operates. Moreover, the intensity of the interpersonal life of the study group has, until recently, tended to outweigh experience in other events in the conference. The introduction of the large-group event, which has no parallel in therapeutic practice as yet, may help to clarify some of the differences between training and therapy.

Any institution that provides the individual with opportunities to learn about himself, and about his behaviour in relation to others and their behaviour in relation to himself, also provides therapy. But this similarity is irrelevant: a therapy group is a group of patients 'taken' by a clinician in a clinical institution; a study group is a group of students 'taken' by a consultant in an educational institution.

CLINIC AND CONFERENCE

The primary task of a clinic is to treat patients. The 'management' of a clinic is responsible, among other things, for seeing that the staff of the clinic are adequately qualified to give the kind of treatment the clinic offers. The staff, whether they treat patients individually or in groups, are responsible for the relevance of the technique they use to the problems they are trying to solve.

The clinic and the members of its staff are responsible for treatment, and therefore for the diagnosis that leads to the kind of treatment given. They are thus responsible for selecting the members of any therapeutic groups that are conducted within the clinic. They are also responsible for what happens to patients, as individuals, in a therapy group. The justification for continuing with a form of treatment for the individual is that it is having a therapeutic effect. The criterion of success is an improvement in his health. I recognize that this is not an easy quality to measure, but whether the patient learns more about interpersonal and intergroup relations as a result of the treatment is not strictly relevant, and whether he becomes a better leader or manager is quite irrelevant unless this can be shown to be related to his health.

The task of a conference of the kind I have been describing is to provide opportunities to learn about leadership and about the human problems of management. Though the provision of opportunities to learn about interpersonal and intergroup relations may be included in the techniques that are used, and some of the techniques may be similar to, or even the same as, those employed in a psychotherapeutic clinic, members are not invited to come for treatment, and hence conference management makes no clinical diagnosis of their need for it.

Conference management accepts responsibility for the repertoire of opportunities that it provides and for the appropriateness of the repertoire for learning about leadership. The qualification for membership of a conference, therefore, is the holding of a job that involves, or will involve, leadership and management. In this statement I am using the terms leadership and management in the same broad sense that I have used throughout. In this sense, any job that involves supervision of the work of others or a professional relationship with others is a job that involves leadership. The wide differences between jobs, and their meaning for conference design, I will discuss in a later section of this chapter. In short, qualification for membership is that the member is doing a job or is in training to do a job for which this kind of experience is appropriate. For these reasons, selection for membership is solely on the basis of the job that the potential member is doing, or going to do, when he applies.

Conference management assumes that those who attend the conferences are mature adults who have taken a conscious decision to try to learn from the opportunities provided. There may be some who have been sent by their organizations and have come unwillingly, but at the time of application the staff group is unlikely to know this and to be able to take cognizance of it. It is a problem of the relations between the unwilling attenders and the organizations that send them – a problem that in the long run conference learning may help them to solve. Clearly, however, if the organizations that send them do so because they are in need, or are believed to be in need, of therapy, they have sent them to the wrong institution. In short, it is no reason for confusing the primary tasks of clinic and conference that some of the same forces are released in the events of a conference as are released in a clinical setting.

THE CHANCE OF STRESS

Nevertheless, in spite of what has been said above, the question of selection criteria for membership of this kind of conference has still not been adequately answered. Modern techniques for management selection use clinical judgements about applicants' suitability to tolerate the stresses and strains of the jobs for which they are applying. And it has often been suggested that a clinical judgement should be made about the suitability of the individual for the kinds of intensive experience that he may go through at a conference. It would be idle to pretend, however, that even

157

the most modern techniques for management selection can ensure that mistakes are not made; or that techniques used to select men and women for professional or other kinds of work in the social services always eliminate those who are not fitted for the tasks they will have to undertake. It is unlikely, therefore, that even an elaborate procedure would eliminate those for whom conference experience is overstressful.

In short, reliance on the job the applicant is doing is not more than a rough safeguard against his finding a conference too disturbing. As yet, however, we have found no practical alternative. Even apart from the time and cost of elaborate selection and rejection procedures, it would be difficult to justify their use for so short a conference. They would assume too great an importance in relation to the event they were intended to select for.

Members, therefore, have to accept some risk that they will find conference experience too stressful; but this does not absolve the staff from the responsibility for dealing with those who do. Before discussing some practical implications, I would like to make four general points:

(a) Any form of education entails risk, not only with regard to what it teaches, but with regard to what it leaves untaught. Individuals vary in their ability to tolerate stress. An institution that guaranteed that the least tolerant of its members would not find the experience overstressful would do little for the majority.

(b) No institution that aims to provide opportunities to learn about the stresses of interpersonal and intergroup relationships can achieve its aim without being stressful, however protected the environment.

(c) To avoid problems in human relationships is often as damaging to those relationships as to try, however ineptly, to solve them. Every individual has a right to his own defences, to choose the problem rather than the solution. But if he works with others, they too have rights; and one of those rights is the expectation that their leader will not use them to act out his own personal problems in a destructive way.

(d) Just as most individuals who are effective change their job – both its terms of reference and ways of doing it – to suit themselves, so most jobs impose constraints on their performers. The constraints arise in society, in the institution in which the job exists, and in the immediate work group, as well as in the individual himself. For most people, coming to terms with the constraints causes stress, and the stress has to be dealt with in some way. In other words, stress, and coming to terms with it, are an inevitable part of our way of living. Conferences to learn about ways of coming to terms with stress are not the only cause of stress; they provide opportunities to explore ways of dealing with what already exists, and what, in a modern complex society, is increasing.

Those who become casualties owing to intolerance of stress behave in many different ways – some more disturbing than others. Some have stayed in the conference; others have left before the end, sometimes to return, sometimes not; and there are also those who apply to come but do not appear at all. Some of the casualties are due to circumstances that have nothing to do with the conference; others, though often rationalized as being the result of external circumstances, can be ascribed to the stress induced by the conference.

At earlier conferences we appear, in retrospect, to have assumed that though a drop-out of members was to be expected up to the moment that the conference started, no one would leave during the conference itself. We anticipated possible withdrawals for a period of time, and the mid-conference break offered an opportunity for withdrawal, but we do not appear to have anticipated actual leaving. At least, staff reaction on the first occasion that it happened – a sense of unforeseen disaster – suggests that it might have been feared but not prepared for. Experience of other institutions suggests, however, that the normal process of institutional turnover is seldom entirely suspended, and though for a comparatively short conference continuous attrition would be suspicious, it is now accepted, if only because we recognize that part of the programme is an export process, that some members may leave before the end.

Withdrawal from a situation can take many forms, all the way from remaining bodily present without participation, to actual leaving. The problem for conference management is to care adequately for the individuals concerned without being too greatly distracted from primary task performance. Those who leave, leave; as individuals they move out of the boundaries of the conference and hence out of the area of responsibility of conference management. Those who stay may attempt to lead management and the conference into a redefinition of the primary task as that of caring for casualties at the expense of the healthy members who are there to learn, not about therapy, but about leadership and management. This is not to say that members of the staff responsible for the management of conferences of this kind do not care about individual members who come to them. They do care, very much so, but the very task they are trying to carry out precludes them from caring for one individual at the expense of the conference as a whole. The conference as a whole is their primary concern. If psychiatric cover is provided in a conference, it is for the sake of the conference and not just for the sake of individual members.

A conference management that creates situations in which stress and strain are inevitable always has to face the possibility that some members, and not only the members of the conference, but staff as well, will be unable to tolerate them; that for some the protection of the conference institution will be insufficient. But breakdowns and withdrawals also occur in other institutions than conferences for studying problems of leadership and management. And dealing with such problems is one of the tasks of leadership. In this sense every leader or manager has to be a 'therapist' of at least sufficient sensitivity to make judgements about when to contain the casualties within his organization, when to call in specialist help, and when, for the sake of the other members of the organization as well as of the organization itself, to remove the casualties. In any changing environment casualties are likely to occur: managers who cannot cope with new technologies, or cannot accept the consequences for themselves of changes in organization; those who, for a variety of reasons, lose their competence. The problem in many institutions is not so much to avoid casualties as to deal with them in the way that causes least damage to the institution and least harm to those who fail.

When a member leaves, or is disturbed by, the conference, it soon becomes obvious to all members. There is inevitably a questioning, not only of the way the staff deal with the particular problem, but more generally of their qualifications for running the conference at all. This is a major testing time for member-staff relationships. It is also a time that provides an opportunity for learning about one of the major stresses of management. Though staff always hope that no serious problems will arise, if they do it is important that their causes and results should be studied by the conference, that the learning opportunity, however painful, should not be missed.

It is common experience that what happens to those who leave an institution voluntarily, or are forced to leave, has effects on those who stay (Rice and Trist, 1952). In an institution in which interpersonal and intergroup relations are the objects of study, the effects are profound. Whatever the apparent cause of leaving, those left behind cannot help but examine in what way their own behaviour has led to the rejection, either of themselves by the leaver or of the leaver by themselves. Questioning staff responsibility for a leaving, and staff qualifications for creating a situation that results in a leaving, is one way of avoiding questioning the responsibility of others, of projecting onto the staff any guilt about the lack of consideration with which the leaver may have been treated.

During the course of the conference, in study groups, in the large group, and in the intergroup exercise, members have become aware of the hostility inherent in the ordinary human relationships of individuals and groups. They have become aware of the suppressed fear of the potential destructiveness of aggression. If the leaving occurs at the point where they have just begun to believe that aggression can be constructive as well as destructive, the belief is likely to be short-lived, and the painful learning has to begin again. It is indeed notable that those who leave towards the end of a conference, whatever the reason, cause far less disturbance than those who leave part-way through.

CONFERENCE DESIGN

Even though I have tried in this chapter to differentiate between institutions whose primary task is education and those whose primary task is therapy, I believe I have also shown that, in practice, the distinction is not always clear. Among the other tasks of leaders and managers of any kind of institution are the recruitment and conservation of the resources of the institution. They are responsible for the promotion and protection of those they lead. Training is an essential part of their task, and where training crosses over to therapy is seldom a clearly defined boundary. If this is true for leaders and managers, in any kind of institution, it is also true that, for those whose profession is therapeutic or educational, the borderline between therapy or education and leadership or management is obscure. The extent, for example, to which a doctor 'manages' his patient – except in surgery – may be limited, but there can be little doubt that, in treating him, he is always trying to lead him. And every doctor has to manage the institution of his practice. In the same way a teacher must both lead and manage his class, even though in the school he may have few 'administrative' duties.

This broad concept of the role of leader has enabled us, so far, to invite to the same conferences managers of industry and commerce, administrators, members of the staff of educational institutions, whether heads

THE CONFERENCE INSTITUTION

or not, prison governors, and those whose task is professional in a therapeutic sense. The primary task of the conference provides appropriate
experiences for all. With further sophistication in conference design, however, I believe that we shall need to take account of the differences in
members' jobs not only in the work of application groups, but in the
design of other conference events as well.

An indication of developments along these lines can already be seen in
different ideas concerning the conduct of the intergroup exercise. In
Chapter 7 I described the kind of exercise I direct. In it I lay particular
emphasis on the relations between the staff group – conference management – and the members, those who, however temporarily, are members
of the institution managed. The structure of the exercise, and the roles
taken by director and consultants, are consistent with the dynamics of
management-subordinate relationships: 'line' and 'staff' functions, inter-
departmental rivalries, joint consultation, and, in general, the problems
that always arise among individuals and groups and the legislative and
executive systems of any organized institution. This slant is a reflection
of my own interest in theories of organization and, more abstractly, in
the interdependence of the personality and the structural and cultural
variables of social institutions.

Those of my colleagues whose primary interests are in the technical
problems of professional practice have not always agreed with the direction
I have given to the conference in general or to the intergroup exercise in
particular. I now think that our differences have been due mainly to our
lack of precision in the definition of the conference task – to the too broad
meaning given to the concept of leadership and management, and hence
to the primary tasks of the various events of the conference. I still believe
that the design of the intergroup exercise I have described is the best we
have so far achieved – I must do so, otherwise I could not direct it – but
this is true only if the task of the conference is as I have defined it – to
provide opportunities to learn about leadership.

On the most recent non-residential course in London, my colleagues
Isabel Menzies and Pierre Turquet redesigned and ran the intergroup
exercise. There was no staff group as such, nor a director of the exercise
for that matter, but only consultants to groups and to intergroup meetings. The exercise started and finished with plenary sessions. In the first
plenary, members received a one-page instruction sheet identifying consultants and rooms (consultants were already there), and giving the times
of sessions; in the second, the consultant to intergroup meetings (Pierre

Turquet) explored the 'here and now' of that meeting, as he had done at the first. He gave no review. The instruction sheet, which was given to members as they started, carried no explanation of the kind of exercise it was (other than its title) and no description of the kinds of problem to be encountered. It concluded with the words, 'The exercise has now started'. This technique was closer to that of the study and the large group than to the technique used in the intergroup exercise at the residential conferences.

On this occasion I acted as consultant to one of the groups. I believe that I learnt a lot about intergroup relations, and so, it seemed to me, did the members. But, at present, I am inclined to think that such an exercise is more appropriate to a conference designed for the needs of professional advisers than to one designed for leaders or managers in the narrower sense of those terms. In the former type, emphasis would be on the understanding of interpersonal and intergroup relations for their own sake rather than for their impact on leadership and management. However, it is not easy to compare this recent exercise with the earlier ones described, because other important differences between residential conferences and non-residential courses would have to be considered. Some of these will be discussed in Chapter 14. Here it is sufficient to say that, at a residential conference, management-member relationships, as distinct from consultant-member relationships, are a more vivid living experience than they are on a non-residential course. On the latter, except for the opening and review plenaries, members have little or no contact with management as such and hence are not preoccupied with the way the course, as a whole, is being run.

With more experience and, I hope, more technical skill and sophistication in conference design, new conferences and courses, which may still use the same or similar techniques, will differentiate tasks and their memberships more precisely.

CHAPTER 13

Institutional Reproduction

The difficulty of differentiating between training and therapy led us, in our early conference, to insist that:

> 'Study Groups should be conducted only by those who have themselves had experience of psycho-analysis . . . . Experience shows that it takes clinical experience and clinical sensitivity to conduct a group in such a way that it steers clear of becoming member- rather than group-centred' (Trist and Sofer, 1959).

Because the only way a consultant could find out what was happening in a group was by examining how he himself felt and why he felt it, he had to know sufficient about himself and about his own feelings to be able to use them for the benefit of the group. At the time, the study group was the focus of conference life; neither the large group nor the intergroup exercise had been added to the programme. Moreover, this was the first conference of its kind, and it is a long-established practice in the Institute that the staff for a first attempt are always the most highly qualified we have. Not only does this ensure that the maximum technical skill available is brought to bear in the event as it happens, but in the design of subsequent events we have the best experience we can find to draw on.

The restriction did, however, make staff recruitment difficult for subsequent conferences. Practising psycho-analysts cannot move far from their practices, nor can they take much time away from their patients except at normal holiday times. Furthermore, since in the United Kingdom psycho-analysis is available only in a few areas, both times and locations for conferences and courses that needed either psycho-analysts or their analysands were severely limited. While this policy continued, full staff roles for conferences and courses outside London would always be confined to individuals who had many years' experience of analysis, and were both able and willing to learn the new group techniques. There appeared to be very few such people available. In these circumstances it did not appear that the methods of training that were being developed could spread very far or very widely, except as a research instrument. We had to think again.

In America, the main developments in human relations training have been undertaken by social psychologists, not clinicians, and in Great Britain more and more conferences and courses were being started without clinically qualified group-takers. Some members who attended our own early conferences used their experiences to set up training activities on similar lines, notably in industry and in the universities. Some were successful; others, however, got into trouble with participants or colleagues, or both. The trouble appeared to stem from two causes: either the 'trainers' stirred up more emotional conflict among the participants than they were willing to face themselves; or they did not appreciate that to provide adequate security both for themselves and for participants the training institution itself had to be secure. Experiments carried out without the knowledge of superiors and colleagues, or without their understanding the potential disturbances that could result, were regarded less as evolutionary than as revolutionary processes. In some cases they were ruthlessly suppressed.

More importantly, our conferences had been started, and continued, in collaboration with the Adult Education Department of the University of Leicester. Psycho-analysis was not available in Leicester. Had full staff membership (in those days synonymous with study-group-taking) remained confined to those with long experience of analysis, then only members of the university who had had the opportunity of adequate personal analysis before taking up their posts in Leicester would have been able to qualify. It seemed inappropriate to pretend to build a collaborative institution with a university that did not, and does not, require any such qualification for membership of its own staff. Indeed, the insistence, on the one hand, of clinical qualifications for full staff membership of the conference, and the attempt, on the other, to build a joint institution with a university whose members would, for the most part, be denied the opportunity of taking full staff roles would inevitably add to the existing confusion between training and therapy. If, after conference staff roles had been tested out clinically by qualified persons, the evidence confirmed that they should be undertaken only by individuals with 'many years of experience of analysis', then it seemed that real collaboration would be impossible.

These problems were discussed on the executive committee through two conferences, and the steps that had been taken to make further training available were reviewed. We had already provided intermittent supervision sessions for members of university staffs who had started various forms of study group in their own courses (Richardson, 1963), and who travelled long distances each week for these sessions. In addition, at conferences, members of university staffs had taken roles as observers in study groups, both participant and non-participant. Sessions in which they had so participated were followed by discussions with the consultant about what had happened and why the consultant had spoken and behaved as he had. (These training sessions, it should be added, were also of considerable value to consultants. They had to think about their own role, and articulate the reasons why they took it as they did.) These discussions, and the further training already provided, in their turn led to more thinking about the conferences and their purposes, the results of which I have described in earlier chapters.

The assumptions about qualifications for staff membership were re-examined; as was the kind of training that would be required if the earlier criteria were to be abandoned. We also examined the possible effects of the contemplated changes in conference structure, which would, we believed, increase the security obtainable from the institution. We made the hypothesis that the steps we had already taken to define the overall primary task of the conference and the sub-tasks of events, to strengthen the role of conference director, and to improve the executive power of management would go some way towards this. These steps, we believed, would reduce some of the need for security that could be found only in the clinical qualifications of individual staff members. The result of this thinking was that for the 1962 conference the executive committee took two critical decisions:

(a) Those members of university staffs who had already had supernumerary staff roles at conferences, had used similar techniques in their own courses, and had subsequent training, would become consultants to study groups under supervision.

(b) We would create an advanced training group.

THE ADVANCED TRAINING GROUP

The advanced training group, membership of which was by invitation, was intended primarily for those who were expected to become members of the future conference staff. Invitations were therefore extended mainly to members of the University of Leicester and the Tavistock Institute. Members of what was then called the Prison Commission were also invited, since that body had sent so many of its staff to the conferences and had expressed interest in further training. The main qualification for membership of the advanced training group was previous attendance at a conference as a member, and the individual's subsequent explicit interest and demonstrated skill in using the methods of the conference in his own job.

As soon as we had decided that members of university staffs should take study groups, we realized that we would probably have to discontinue the role of observer in the groups to which they acted as consultants. The problems of acting as consultant to a study group for the first time are difficult enough without the additional complication of observation. This meant that our reorganization had left us without places at the conference for people who wished to attend, but whose qualifications made it inappropriate that they should come as ordinary members even though they could not take staff roles at once. For example, some who may have held staff status in training laboratories in America and elsewhere are nevertheless interested in enlarging their experience by attending our conferences and comparing different forms of training. There are also the practising analysts who wish to move into the training field as an addition to their professional experience. However willing staff of other laboratories or analysts may be to attend as ordinary members, their experience and qualifications would inevitably make it difficult for other members to feel at one with them. In default of any other roles, persons who came into this category were offered membership of the advanced training group, in which their experience would be matched at least in part.

Even more importantly, our intention to use the conference institution to provide security meant that we could no longer, as in the past, have supernumerary staff at a conference, that is those without specific and public tasks. Members had to know who the staff were and what their roles and functions were. Observers, research workers, and others with vague titles and indeterminate roles, yet with all the privileges of staff members, would weaken institutional boundaries and hence diminish the capacity of the institution to provide security.

We now had a conference institution that consisted of: first, the staff, all of whom had a number of defined roles, so that none, from the members' point of view, was unaccounted for; second, an advanced training group, with defined qualifications for membership; and third, members. For the first conference incorporating these changes we were uncertain how the advanced training group would fit in, but we assumed that its members would become more identified with staff than with ordinary conference members, and that we should therefore structure the conference in this way. At the opening plenary the staff and members faced each other; the advanced training group members sat together to one side – 'in the choir stalls', became the phrase. They were made members of the staff common room and attended staff meetings. Over the last three conferences there have been some modifications in these arrangements, some on technical grounds, others because of the physical layout of the buildings in which the conferences are held.

The programme, too, has evolved over the last three conferences. While members are in their study groups, the advanced training group has its own study group. Although this group offers an experience that is, in essence, a repetition of a previous study group – not that that in itself is bad – its members are less heterogeneous than are the members of ordinary study groups. Because they are potential members of staff, they have a closer personal relationship with their consultant – Pierre Turquet – than is possible in member study groups; some indeed are his colleagues in the Tavistock Institute and Clinic. This makes the role of consultant to the advanced training group's study group particularly stressful. Equally, however, it places additional stresses on the members of the advanced training group. They have accepted an invitation to go on with this kind of experience. They cannot, therefore, take an escape route open to ordinary members and claim that they did not know what they were in for. They are committed in advance, and their experience is therefore the more intense.

While conference members are in the large-group event, the advanced training group has its own application group. The subjects of discussion are the design and running of conferences and courses; the interpolation, into other kinds of courses, of events to provide opportunities to learn about interpersonal and intergroup relations; the differences and similarities between courses run with single organizations and courses with membership drawn from different organizations. The advanced training group's application group is taken by those members of staff who have been ordinary conference members and subsequently members of an advanced training group, and have already had one year as staff members. Their personal experience of a previous advanced training group is close enough to enable them to know how the members of the current group are feeling, and most of them have been concerned with the introduction of new kinds of training into other organizations. That is the theory. In practice, the first few sessions of the advanced training group's application group suffer – if that is the right word – from the spill-over from the study group; and its task appears to get lost in the adjustment from one kind of event to another. In other words, the application groups of the advanced training group and of the ordinary members suffer from the same disadvantage, but for the advanced training group the experience comes earlier in the conference.

In the intergroup exercise, except on one occasion, the advanced training group has operated as a group. Within the conference it is a recognizable entity. What its members do subsequently is left to them. Except for the time mentioned when, by reason of the structure of the exercise, they could not do so, they have always remained as a group throughout, experiencing in the process all the problems of in-betweenness, common to any intermediate grade in any hierarchy. Members turn to the advanced training group as to a possible alternative to the staff group. If the advanced training group tries to take such a position, it invariably comes under fierce attack from the members. If, on the other hand, the advanced training group tries to join conference members in attacking the staff, it finds itself encouraged but seldom followed. Members usually succeed in splitting the staff and the advanced training group. This does not protect the staff from attempts to split them from each other, nor, however, does it protect the advanced training group from members' attempts to prove the power of the staff group by demonstrating the impotence of the advanced training group. From many points of view, the existence of the advanced training group in the intergroup exercise, as in other parts of the conference, is an added complication for conference management; equally, however, its presence does reflect, in the conference, a common experience in the external world in which relationships between top, middle, and junior groups are frequently even more complicated.

During the application groups for members, the advanced training group is split up and its members take subsidiary staff roles, accepting responsibility, with the consultant, for the conduct of the application groups. In lectures, members of the advanced training group take the same position as that of the staff who attend. They are there as privileged visitors and are not expected to take part in the discussion unless what they have to say helps both platform and audience.

The conferences are for the benefit of members and the task of the staff is to help members. It would be fatal if the members were used or felt they were being used by the staff to enable the advanced training group to get training. For this reason members of the advanced training group arrive ahead of the ordinary members so that they can have their introduction to the conference before the formal opening plenary. And for the same reason there is a special review session between the staff and the advanced training group during a members' free period so that, at the plenary reviews, the staff can concentrate their attention on members' problems.

Nothing is really settled about common rooms. Though, in terms of conference status, those in the advanced training group are between members and staff, they themselves, the staff, and the members identify the group more closely with staff than with members. It is inappropriate, therefore, that the advanced training group should be admitted to the members' common room. But at the first conference that included an advanced training group the staff found that they needed some privacy to deal with their own relationship problems, and there were times when sharing their common room was an embarrassment. This was also felt by the advanced training group, who improvised a common room of their own. At the next conference, because of building alterations in the hall of residence in which the conference was held, there was just no convenient room that was large enough to hold both the staff and the advanced training group. The advanced training group, therefore, had their own common room, as did the staff, and the only common meeting ground was the bar. The advanced training group had no opportunity of meeting members without staff being present, or of meeting staff without members being present.

But this kind of thinking can soon lead to farcical demands: separate common rooms for staff, members, advanced training group, staff and members, staff and advanced training group, members and advanced training group, and finally one for everybody. Sheer economy in the use of the building and, indeed, the practical value of the time that can be spent in common rooms make any extension beyond three unrealistic. At the last conference we once more had a joint common room for the staff and the advanced training group, and set aside a workroom, primarily for the use of staff for staff meetings, but also available for supervision, for meetings of application-group teams and of the advanced training group's application group, and any other like activities. The constraints imposed by accommodation and cost have to be accepted, and within these constraints there has to be freedom to discuss the use to which the accommodation is put. If the use of a joint common room leads to the improvisation of separate meeting places, or to the actual provision of separate meeting places, then this becomes a part of the interpersonal and intergroup relations of staff and advanced training group, and, provided it can be discussed, it can offer learning opportunities for both.

STAFF ROLES UNDER SUPERVISION

The next step after membership of the advanced training group is to be a staff member under supervision. Such staff members normally become consultants to study groups and to application groups. They may also give lectures, and act as observers in the large group.

As soon as possible after each study-group session, consultants meet their supervisor to discuss what has happened in the session. They describe the course of events, how they felt, how they behaved, and what they said. My own experience of acting as a supervisor – and I believe it is the same for my colleagues – is that I find it easier to understand what has happened in a group when I am told about it afterwards than I would have done had I been there. I have a second-hand experience of what I know happens to me only too often: ten minutes after a session is over I see all the things I should have seen at the time. But I believe that discussion is helpful to staff members taking their first study group. Not only does it give them some security but they learn something about their own behaviour, and about the way that this is in part a consequence of what the group is doing to them and in part a consequence of their own attitudes and motives.

Supervision of new staff members who are taking application groups for the first time is not easy. They have usually had ample experience of seminars, tutorials, or case conferences. I have tried to describe earlier why I believe that such previous experience is sometimes unhelpful. The problem is not so much that of helping a new staff member to act as consultant to an application group, as of trying to help him sort out why the group does not appear to be going as well as he expects it to. The experience of senior staff members is that they too consider application groups very difficult to cope with, and frequently find themselves slipping into straightforward teaching roles, rather than trying to help members to apply conference learning to the situations they are describing.

During the intergroup exercise, new staff members form a part of the staff group that remains with the director of the exercise. With him they represent the rump of management. They act as delegates of the staff group in relations with other groups, and as a group receive representatives of member groups.

THE COMPLETION OF STAFF TRAINING

The final step is to full staff membership, which means taking roles as consultants to groups in the intergroup exercise, to the large group, and to application groups, as well as being available for study groups. Both staff under supervision and, still more, full staff members take part in the staff meeting that reviews the conference that has just finished, in the planning of the next conference, and in the choice of their own successors.

The training programme that has now developed for staff membership is thus a four-stage process:

1. Conference membership
2. Membership of an advanced training group
3. Selected staff roles under supervision
4. Full staff roles.

Since there is only one conference a year run by the University of Leicester and the Tavistock Institute in collaboration, it can take a long time to complete the process. However, as will be seen below, other developments in collaboration with other institutions are now starting, and more opportunities for quicker progress through the various stages, and for experimenting with different kinds of training, will become available. The executive committee of the Leicester/Tavistock joint institution intends to build up to a fully qualified staff of about twenty, mainly drawn from universities and other non-clinical institutions. It is necessary to have about that number in order to allow for normal staff turnover – particularly in such an intermittent institution – and for the temporary lack of availability of some. This means that once they have completed the four stages of training, new members of staff normally expect to stand down for a year or two to make room for others to be trained. We do not wish to go further than this, if it can be avoided, however, since staff would not get adequate opportunities to renew their experience. While only the one collaborative conference existed, the limitations on staff size would have restricted the opportunities that were available for further training. For this reason alone, apart from others, we welcome the growth of new joint institutions.

INSTITUTIONAL REPRODUCTION

In 1963, the Reverend Bruce Reed, Director of Christian Teamwork, who had attended one of the Leicester/Tavistock conferences as a member of the advanced training group, asked the Institute to collaborate with his organization in setting up similar kinds of conferences for men and women in the church and in industry. The purpose of the conferences is to help with the problems that beset practising Christians in a modern technological society. A short experimental conference was held in November 1963, and a second one, of six days, in June 1964. As a result of of these experiments the conferences are now becoming established, and there is already beginning an interchange of staff between the Leicester/Tavistock and the Christian Teamwork conferences.

About the same time as we were arranging the November Christian Teamwork conference, Dr Margaret Rioch of the Washington School of Psychiatry, who had also been a member of an advanced training group at Leicester, asked the Institute to organize an additional conference for a group of Americans whom she had interested in the work. They were mainly psychiatrists and psychologists from the Washington School of Psychiatry, the American Army Medical Corps, the National Institute for Mental Health, private practice, and university departments of psychiatry and psychology. This conference, in which a number of European members participated, was held in July 1964.

With both institutions, Christian Teamwork and the Washington School, we have put forward the hypothesis that it would be inappropriate for the Institute to run conferences on their behalf as a continuing project. We have suggested that if work of this kind is to spread, what is needed is the building of joint institutions staffed in the first place by the collaborating organization and the Institute. Subsequently, the collaborating institutions should take over the running of their own conferences or courses, modifying the techniques to suit their own particular needs, Once their own conferences or courses are established, then the joint institutions can be used for the benefit of all collaborating institutions and the Institute to develop new methods and to train new staff. In work of this kind, more perhaps than in any other, a real pooling of experience and skill requires more than an exchange of documents or even of staff. Only by working together on a common problem, in an institution for which a common responsibility is accepted, is there likely to be an adequate exchange.

Simultaneously with these developments there has been an increased demand from individuals in industry, in education, and in other institutions for further training, to enable them to use conference methods or modifications of them in their own organizations. They too would like the experience of conference membership, of the advanced training group, of selected and full staff roles as a means of achieving adequate skills. The increase in the number of joint and independent conference institutions will go a long way towards making this possible without completely abandoning the original purpose of the staff training programme of the Leicester/Tavistock institution – to train staff for its own conferences.

CHAPTER 14

Summary and Future Prospects

Some reasons for the changes in conference design have already been described in earlier chapters: the modification of the intergroup exercise, the introduction of the large-group event and of the advanced training group, the reinforcement of the conference as an institution and the consequent reorganization of programme and management. These changes have resulted in the dropping of external projects for conferences that last only two weeks, the suspension of any follow-up event other than the introduction of an advanced training group, and the omission of special interest sessions. In the first section of this chapter I propose to summarize the concepts on which these developments have been based as a preface to discussions about the differences between residential conferences and non-residential courses; the introduction of this kind of learning opportunity into other kinds of training institution; and the problems of research into conference and course effectiveness.

SUMMARY OF CONCEPTS USED IN DEVELOPING CONFERENCE DESIGN

Love and hate, like and dislike, amity and hostility, trust and distrust, all for the same person, are indissoluble components of any meaningful human relationship. Because relations between leaders and followers must be based on their mutual dependence, the stresses and conflicts caused by these antithetic feelings have to be dealt with, suppressed, or otherwise controlled whenever decisions have to be taken. Any understanding of the problems of leadership must therefore take account of the potential destructiveness of the hostility inherent in all interpersonal and intergroup relations.

The individual, the small group, and the large group have been described as structures of increasing complexity. The individual has an internal personal world comprised of whole and part objects dynamically related to each other and to the personality pattern that results from them, and an ego function that relates this inner world to the external world of reality. The internal environment of the small group is made up of the interpersonal relations of its members, and their overlapping images of the group task, structure, and culture. Group leadership, however transient and changing, is required to relate the group to its external environment. A large group is made up of so many individuals that they cannot maintain face-to-face relationships. They may be related to each other in both formal and informal structures. The large group has both a complex interpersonal life and an intergroup life of its own. It too requires leadership to control transactions between itself and its environment. The environments of the individual, the small group, and the large group are composed of other individuals and groups, but any individual is likely to be a member of more than one small group in any large group and of more than one large group in any environment.

For the performance of any task some form of organization, however rudimentary, is required, if only to ensure that resources are available for performance and that operations are carried out in proper sequence. It is obvious that the most appropriate organization is that which best fits task performance. What is less often recognized, however, is that an essential prerequisite for organization-building is therefore the definition of the task and the examination of the constraints on task performance. This should be followed by the identification of the dominant import-conversion-export process by which the task is performed, and on which the organization can then be modelled.

The function of leadership is to control transactions between internal and external environments. This function, on whatever scale it is exercised, from the individual to large structured institutions, involves whether explicitly or not the location and definition of the boundary between what is inside and what is outside, the management of the internal environment so that transactions can take place across the boundary, and the control of those transactions for the benefit – however benefit is calculated – of what is inside. At the conscious level, leadership is task-centred and the boundaries controlled are rational; at the unconscious level, the leader expresses feelings and emotions, and the boundaries, which may or may not coincide with task boundaries, are irrational. At the conscious level the leader is appointed or elected; at the unconscious level he takes or is put into a role, of which he may or may not be aware, that requires him to go into collusion with the unconscious strivings of those inside the boundary. From the point of view of those inside a given boundary, therfore, more than one leader or one kind of leadership may be required at any given time: to lead in the performance of the manifest task and to give expression to group emotions that are inconsistent with this performance. The first leadership is concerned with transactions between the internal and the external environments, the second with transactions across internal boundaries.

These propositions may be stated more generally (cf. p. 14 above):

If p represents the internal world of the individual,
  P the leadership function exercised by the ego, and
  E_P the external environment of the individual,

then we can write:

$$P = f(p, E_P) \tag{1}$$

If this is now extended to groups and g represents the interpersonal life of a group, then:

$$g = f(P_1, P_2, P_3, \ldots P_n)$$

where $P_1, P_2, P_3, \ldots P_n$ are the members of the group.

If G is the manifestation of group leadership in relation to E_G, the external environment of the group, we can write as in (1):

$$G = f(g, E_G) \tag{2}$$

In the same way, if l represents the interpersonal and intergroup life of a large group comprising a number of individuals $(P_1, P_2, \ldots P_n)$ and a number of small groups $(G_1, G_2, G_3, \ldots G_n)$, and L the manifestation of large-group leadership in relation to E_L, the external environment of the group, then:

$$l = f(P_1, P_2, P_3, \ldots P_n; G_1, G_2, G_3, \ldots G_n)$$

and

$$L = f(l, E_L) \tag{3}$$

These equations (1), (2), and (3) are the equivalent of the relationships shown diagrammatically in *Figure 1* (p. 15).

For a structured institution i and I can be substituted for l and L in equation (3). In our conferences the conflicting leadership roles in g are examined in the study group, and those in l in the large group. In the study group the consultant represents G, and in the large group L, in relation to the conference task. The roles taken by Ps in G are examined in the intergroup exercise. I and i are represented throughout the conference by the management function of the staff group, and are examined in the relations within the staff group and between the staff group and the members, both before and during the conference.

The major constraints on task performance, apart from staff qualifications, time, and cost, are the limited extent to which leadership can be taught and the willingness of members to tolerate the pain of learning. The conference can provide only opportunities to learn. The design is therefore based on offering those opportunities in stages that match the increasing complexities of the structures under examination, in an institution that defines the tasks of the various events and controls as firmly as possible the boundaries between them, and between them and other social and administrative activities. The definition of the primary task and the control of the boundaries of the conference institution itself are manifested by the way members are recruited, by the attempt to deal with problems of leaving before the conference ends, and by staff behaviour at the conference.

CONFERENCES AND COURSES

Throughout this account I have, with few exceptions, taken my examples from the two-week residential conferences we have run either in collaboration with the University of Leicester or on our own. I have done this: first, because we have held more conferences of this kind than of any other and hence have more experience and, I hope, knowledge of them; and second, because, until recently, the programmes of other courses or conferences have been derived directly from the two-week residential conferences. Thus the evening courses run in London on one day a week had the same programme as the two-week residential conferences, but stretched out over six months. Some changes in the ordering of events were of course made necessary by our having only two sessions at a time, with a week between pairs of sessions. The maintenance of continuity in any one event from session to session meant that, in the six-month course, only two events could be run in parallel. In the residential conferences four parallel events are in active existence from the fourth day through to the eleventh. Nevertheless, the kinds of events, their general sequence, and the numbers of sessions given to each event were all approximately the same in the two-week residential conferences and the evening courses.

In the experimental four-day conference, run in collaboration with Christian Teamwork, the large-group event and the intergroup exercise were dropped entirely for want of time. Sessions were shortened to one and a quarter hours instead of one and a half; and we worked on a pro-gramme of five working sessions per day instead of four. The conference consisted of opening, study groups, lectures, application groups, and review. In the six-day conference, also run in collaboration with Christian Teamwork, the additional sessions obtained by the extension were used to reintroduce the intergroup exercise as well as to add more study-group sessions and an extra lecture. In future conferences we hope to reintro-duce the large-group event. To do this we shall sacrifice two application-group sessions, and on two days out of six have six working periods instead of five.

The programme of the two-week residential conferences has been based on experience. Evidence for the changes that have been made has been empirical, and though originating mainly in the conferences themselves has also, in part, arisen from the informal communications of ex-members and their colleagues. When we planned the six-month courses and the shorter residential conferences, we recognized that the programme might need to be thought out again, and that the whole conference and course institution could require radical reorganization. But we had too little evidence on which to base major change. So far as we can tell at present, our programme for the residential conferences is sound. There are no obvious faults that need correcting. We are less certain, however, about the non-residential courses. Recruitment is not easy and attendance is irregular. But how far reluctant application and irregular attendance are due to the reality of the difficulties of getting to, and continuing with, a course in the centre of London,[1] and how far to the nature of the course

---

[1] The 1962-1963 course received editorial mention in the *Guardian* as the most ex-pensive evening class in London. The courses and conferences are without subsidy, and the fees charged have to cover not only staff salaries and administrative costs but all overheads, both fixed and variable, as well. By the generosity of foundations and other grant-giving bodies mentioned in the acknowledgements, some bursaries to cover part of the fees are made available to a few non-industrial applicants.

and its programme is, as yet, impossible to say.

In the two years during which the courses have been running we have had three matched pairs of participants in the Leicester conference and the London course. Each pair has come from the same organization. One of each pair has attended the residential conference, the other the non-residential course. Discussions with them afterwards have shown that conference and course are very different in impact:

'I got it over in two weeks. It was tremendous, but I don't think I've remembered so much as John. But I don't think I could stand it stretched out.'

'I found it difficult to concentrate on the course when my mind was still full of what I'd been doing that day and what I'd have to do the next. I may have remembered more, but that's just words.'

From one of a pair who attended the conference:

'It was going back that seemed so strange. After a week it was the conference that became the real world, it was my job that seemed so fantastic. I suppose I've applied a lot of what I learned – at least my colleagues tell me so – but I don't know; they didn't seem connected at the time, and even now, though I can see some parallels, they're only the obvious ones, and I didn't really need a whole fortnight for them.'

And the other member of the same pair:

'The important thing was that I could take it in bits. I'd come with my mind full of a problem, and the next week I'd know if what I'd learned had helped me. Sometimes it did, sometimes it didn't. Sometimes it took longer for the penny to drop.'

One pair not only came from the same organization but did the same job, had the same rank, shared an office, and lived together. They compared notes throughout the whole six-month period and each watched the effect of the conference or course on the other. Their views echoed those I had already heard from other pairs. At the end of a discussion with them, feeling, I suppose, that I still had no starting-point for serious investigation, I said:

'If you had to repeat the experience, which would you choose – conference or course?'

As with one voice, they replied:

'Conference!'

'Course!'

And it was the one who had been on the course who chose the conference and the one who had been on the conference who chose the course. Clearly, the programme, the time, and the location are not the only factors involved; personality too plays its part. And maybe conference and course do provide different experiences. At least those who have attended both, and there are a few, feel it is so, even if they cannot put the difference into words. However, it is probable that a second attendance at the same type of event would provide a different experience too.

In the six-month course, staff as well as members come from, and return to, their ordinary jobs each evening. We have found it impossible to build up and maintain the same kind of tight-knit staff group in a non-residential course as in a residential conference. In a residential conference the staff live, eat, and work together, and have no other duties to perform. They are available for staff meetings and for consultation with each other at all times when they are not taking part in a session. On a course, even finding a time when all staff can be present at once is difficult. Most staff arrive for their particular sessions having just finished another job, and they often have to leave immediately afterwards to attend events connected with their daily work. Occasionally, the staff who are involved on any one evening can meet during the short half-hour interval between the first and second sessions, but those not involved on that evening are seldom available.

Though I have been described as director of the non-residential courses, I too have other things to do during the rest of the week and am frequently preoccupied by them. I do not feel that I have the same kind of control over the course as an institution as I have in the case of the residential conference. More formally, it is impossible to define the boundaries of the course as precisely as those of a conference, and hence control of the boundary conditions is inevitably weakened. Though I maintain close contacts with my colleagues during the course, the contacts are not only about the course, but about all the other jobs in which we work together as well. With members I have far less exchange. In effect, the difference is that in a residential conference the boundaries of the conference and of the institution in which it is held coincide; on a course they do not. A course is a part of an institution that carries out other tasks as well. The institution which members join temporarily, and from which therefore they obtain some of their security, is the institution in which the course is held, not the institution of the course.

To try to deal with some of these problems, on the first course we did not set aside a room for the sole use of members between sessions, but staff and members took coffee and drinks together. After a short time it became clear that this arrangement had destroyed a major advantage of separate accommodation and had introduced a major disadvantage. The advantage destroyed was that of privacy, which allowed members to talk freely about the staff, and staff to talk about members. The disadvantage was that the coffee-break became a kind of communications centre, but the communications that passed, because they were social and not professional, could not be used in the course – at least, could not be used without other modifications to course design.

I now feel that the role of director of a course is quite different from the role of director of a conference. In the pre-course phase, executive direction is required, if only to bring the course into being; but once it has started all that is required is an administrator, and perhaps a non-executive chairman of the staff group. It is not so desirable, in comparison with the residential conference, that such a chairman should keep aloof from course events; he can participate like the other staff members; in addition, other staff members can take leading roles in those events that in the residential conferences are taken by the director – the intergroup exercise, the opening and review plenaries. In other words, the role of director is not required as a continuing symbol of course leadership and management.

The more imporatnt implication is that we cannot hope to create a course institution, with properties of its own that would provide opportunities for learning. For this purpose the course would have to be studied in the context of the Tavistock Institute itself, and this study, though perhaps useful and not uninteresting, would require more time and other techniques than can be offered on a course.

We have not abandoned the idea of courses such as those we have now run for two years. But we are at present experimenting with a series of separate courses – of study groups, application groups, lectures, and intergroup exercises. Individuals can elect to attend for one type of event only, or can attend several different kinds of event. There will be no unifying course institution as such. With this experience we shall be in a better position to review the programme and organization required for an integrated course.

182

THE INTRODUCTION OF LEARNING FOR LEADERSHIP
INTO OTHER EDUCATIONAL INSTITUTIONS

The words 'leader' and 'follower' are given wide meaning in this book. Teachers, doctors, lawyers, and other professional workers, as well as officers, managers, and supervisors, are all presumed to have to display qualities of leadership in their work. Most leaders exercise their skill intuitively as part of their personalities. But the rapid changes in the social and technological conditions of modern society make the role of leader, in almost every walk of life, an increasingly difficult one. There is therefore an urgent need to provide more opportunities for men and women in management, administration, and professional work to learn, and to practise, the skills required. It seems only reasonable to expect those educational institutions responsible for training future managers, administrators, and professional workers to do more than they have done in the past to provide their students with experience of the interpersonal and intergroup problems of leadership, in situations in which they can learn from it.

There is, as yet, no one agreed method by which this learning can best be accomplished; nor is it likely, or indeed desirable, that, at the present stage of our knowledge of human behaviour, agreement will be reached. But those who have attempted to introduce the methods outlined in this book, or variations of them, into established training institutions have had a mixed success. Failures have been variously attributed to the lack of skill of the trainers and to the opposition of colleagues and superiors. I suspect that more trouble has arisen from lack of experience in institution-building than from the unskilful use of training techniques.

In residential conferences, organized and managed by independent institutions, it is difficult enough to provide adequate security for members. It can be done only by firm control of the boundary conditions of the conference institution and of the events that make up the programme. Such control is made more difficult if the conference is a part of, and dependent on, a larger educational institution. In non-residential courses there are added problems caused by breaking-up and leaving at the end of every session or group of sessions. I have discussed in the previous section some of the consequences of this in the courses run by the Tavistock Institute. The Institute itself has to sanction the courses and provide the members with institutional protection. This, however, it can do, since the courses arise directly from its work and policy.

But if the leaders of an institution do not actively support the introduction of new techniques or, still worse, are hostile to them, then both the staff and their students are in jeopardy. The members of staff who are trying to maintain the integrity of a course boundary so that the interpersonal and intergroup problems of authority relations can be studied are in a well-nigh impossible position if they are themselves in difficulties with their own employers. Under such conditions the students could hardly fail to make use of conflicts between the staff and their superiors to act out their own hostilities to the staff. This in its turn is only too likely to aggravate any existing rivalries between colleagues on the staff and to lead to still more higher management interference.

The conclusion can only be that support from 'top management' is essential. The difficulty is to obtain not only support for the first attempts but also toleration of the mistakes that will inevitably be made. Talking and writing about the kind of 'training' involved are of limited value. The conferences and courses prove this. Perhaps the best that can be hoped for is a 'protected experiment', preferably in an off-centre area of the institution's work. By a protected experiment, I mean one in which the decision is taken in advance not to interfere with the experiment while it is going on, and not to make any judgement about its results until some time after it is over.

Even with top management support the problems of integrating the methods of the conferences and courses outlined here with the syllabuses of other kinds of training can be formidable. There is a high probability of confusion between different kinds of training, of displacing hostilities from one kind of training onto another, and hence of fighting between the wrong people and about the wrong things. The chance that the stress of learning about interpersonal and intergroup relations might interfere with effective learning of other subjects must also be taken into account. As, of course, must the possibility that the resolution of some of the conflicts and the working-through of some of the hostilities may make other activities infinitely more productive. With our present limited knowledge, I would recommend that 'learning for leadership' should not be intermingled with other subjects, but should be a course on its own, at a time when no other training is being carried out. Because I believe that the chance of its helping other learning is far greater than that of its hindering it, 'learning for leadership' should come at the beginning of the longer training programme in which it is included. If time permits it should be repeated before the end.

If the educational institution into which the new methods are to be introduced is itself a part of a different kind of institution – an industrial company or a government department, for example – the potential difficulties are increased. Training departments in institutions whose primary task is not education, but profit-making or service, are, like other educational institutions, change-producing agencies; but since they do not carry out a part of the primary task of the institution to which they belong, they constitute a service function only. The top management from which they must get their support has, as its major preoccupation, a different primary task. Any training activities, particularly those concerned with management development, that appear to interfere with, or to jeopardize, performance of that primary task are likely to be resisted, if not suppressed entirely.

Clearly, the best initial protection for the introduction of new methods of learning for leadership is the conviction of top management that the new methods will enhance the institution's primary task performance. Such conviction comes most readily from personal experience. Without this, 'protected experiment' is essential.[1]

COMPREHENSIVE RESEARCH

At times, colleagues both in the Tavistock Institute and elsewhere have brought considerable pressure to bear on the members of the staff group to get them to initiate systematic research work in the conference. There have been, and are, divergent views even within the staff group. The demands have always been for research into study-group processes. We have frequently been asked why we have not made use of such established research techniques as content and process analysis, before and after measures of attitude change, and comparative studies of the behaviour of differently constituted groups; why we have not installed recording devices and one-way screens for detached evaluation and observation.

My own resistance to the introduction of research has been based on a number of grounds. I have always believed, and still believe, that it could be dangerously misleading to introduce research only into the small-group activities of the conference. An analogy from the Rorschach technique of personality investigation may illustrate: I feel that research only into study groups would be the equivalent of a careful examination of the small details and an ignoring of the whole and large detail. In other words,

1 Argyris (1962) gives a detailed case history of such an experiment.

I believe that what is first required is a study of the total conference and of the place of the events in it. Only when they have been adequately defined and realized does it seem appropriate to study interactions in small-group activities. Without a study of the whole first, there are two dangers: that inadequate account will be taken of the setting in which the activities occur and false extrapolations made; and that, from the study of small-group behaviour, inappropriate generalizations will be made about large- group and intergroup behaviour.

The task of the study group is to examine its own behaviour as it happens. To maximize the performance of that task, the boundary of the group has to be precisely defined and firmly controlled. Once microphones or one-way screens were installed they would permit what happened inside to be heard and seen outside; the boundary of the group would be breached, and both definition and control weakened. I have not objected to a qualified consultant's introducing his own tape recorder into a group, if this technique helps him to perform his task more effectively. Once a consultant has been appointed he is entirely responsible for what happens and has full authority to determine his own methods of work. If he takes the tape recorder in himself, and is responsible for the recording, he is still in control of the group boundary.

My own experience of recording group meetings has not been fruitful. I have not attempted it in conferences, but I have tried it in other settings in which the interpersonal relations of those with whom I have been working have had to be explored. Even when the presence of the recorder had apparently been ignored, I did not find the transcripts very useful in helping me to help my clients; the recording could not, of course, reveal all the behaviour that seemed at the time to be much more significant than what was said. More importantly, and this may well be a personal idiosyncrasy, the very fact that a recording was being made meant that, without my realizing it, I did not concentrate as hard as I should have done on what was happening while it was happening. If I did not understand something at the time, unconsciously I consoled myself with the belief that I could always pick it up later from the tape. Even if I did this, it was usually too late to be of much practical value. I find, too, that taking notes at such a meeting puts the notes between me and what I am trying to grapple with. The very act of writing provides me with an escape from the immediate present.

As against these objections I have to accept, of course, that recollections of what happened in any group, on any occasion, are far less reliable as records of content than would be recordings taken on the spot. On balance, I have been prepared to accept the distortion of a subsequent account rather than take the risk of distortion of the immediate event.

But my major objection to research work so far has been based on the need to defend a developing and growing institution from premature interference. I have discussed in earlier chapters some of the relationship problems of the staff group and some of the difficulties of the role of director. I have seen as my most important task the building of the conference institution, which permits the members of the staff to give absolute priority to the needs of the conference members. In the early stages of this building process, the introduction of research – however important it may be for the future – would, I believe, have jeopardized this priority. Once it is secure, however, research becomes possible.

Whether research is carried out or not, the conferences will continue to change and to grow: these processes cannot be halted. What we must now develop is a systematic programme of research that will enable us to take better informed decisions about the optimum directions of change and growth.

AN OUTLINE PROGRAMME FOR RESEARCH

I suggest that the first research objective should be to delineate conference boundaries more precisely and to measure the control over them. This means that research should first start outside the conference, both before and after it, in the source of its imports and in the destination of its exports. A large part of conference learning takes place unconsciously. This learning is not readily available as research data but can be reached only by highly skilled interviewing over time. Even much of the conscious learning takes place in post-conference reflection and in the encountering of homologous or analogous situations elsewhere. This means that attempts to discover what change has taken place at the conference itself may ignore much of the relevant data.

The first research task would be in three steps. The first step would be to interview, either individually or in groups, a sample of those who have received an announcement of a conference, to investigate how decisions are made about whether to attend or who should be selected to attend. As a second step, a sample of those who registered as members would then be seen at regular intervals before the conference started, to try to discover to what extent the initial decision to attend had to be remade, as attitudes towards the conference change in the interval between booking and actual attendance. These interviews would also endeavour to delineate respondents' perceptions of social relationships in general, and their attitudes towards authority, both upwards and downwards, in particular. They would explore feelings about actual superiors, colleagues, and subordinates, and attempt to differentiate between role and personal relationships. How respondents saw themselves and their task, now and in prospect, would be explored.

The third step would pick up this sample after the conference and follow the ex-members through until any changes in the perceptions of themselves and others as a result of their experience had crystallized, or at least become stable enough to justify the assumption that further change would be predictable. If this first objective could be combined with before and after assessments of job performance by the individual himself, his colleagues, and his subordinates, it would of course enhance the value of the data; but I would resist any research activity that jeopardized the security of the member after the conference or the confidentiality of its proceedings while it was on.

The value of this first piece of research would be enhanced by duplicating it for non-residential courses, or for residential conferences with different membership compositions.

The second research task would be to examine the processes by which a sample of members crossed the conference boundaries from outside to inside, passed through the various events in the conference, and then left it to return to their normal work. Again, interviewing techniques would be used. The first objective would be to discover any discrepancies between anticipation immediately before the conference began and feelings immediately after it had opened; the second, to discover how far experience in one event is carried over into others in a cumulative learning process, or how far change from one kind of event to another confuses rather than helps; the third, to investigate discrepancies in feeling just before the end of the conference, and immediately on return home.

It may be that for some the conference would be found to have started before they arrived; others would not feel it had begun until they had been at the conference for some days. For some it may end before the closing date, for others it may persist after the return home. This information is of importance for conference design. At present we tend to plunge the members in as soon as they arrive on the assumption that, having actually come to the conference, they want to get on with it. Even if this is true, it may still not be the best way of providing opportunities to learn. Similarly, at the end, the length of time necessary to prepare for the return home needs verification.

We already know that experience in one event affects behaviour in others. That is a matter of observation, but whereas the carry-over into some events, for example into application groups, appears to confuse and may hinder learning, into others, such as the lecture series, the carry-over appears to enhance learning. We do not know to what extent this phenomenon is universal, or whether it applies only to certain classes of member or only to individuals. Nor do we know enough about the optimum dosage – how many sessions of each kind of event provides the best mix; how much free time for digestion and relaxation is required. The answers we have at present have been reached experimentally, but there has been little measurable control over the experiments; the evidence has been mainly staff conviction based on experience at consecutive conferences.

When the first short conference with Christian Teamwork was being planned, there were, for example, grave doubts among the staff about the value of a series of study groups in a conference that could last only four days. It was suggested that, if we were to have study groups at all, then we should continue them to the end of the conference (in order to fit more in) and abandon the principle that because they were unique to the conference they had to finish before the end. We did use study groups, we had fewer of them than we have ever had before, and we stopped them before the end of the conference. The experiment worked – at least to the extent that the director and staff of Christian Teamwork have continued with them. But we do not know whether a different programme would, in the time available, have provided more learning opportunities.

When these questions have been answered, we shall be able to assess more accurately the effects of the introduction into the conference of research workers and research apparatus. We may then begin to find answers to the more complex questions about why particular events have the effect they appear to have, what parts of them are remembered consciously, and what parts appear to effect changes in behaviour though they are not consciously assimilated. We could then with some confidence introduce the more sophisticated research techniques into the events themselves.

APPENDIX

REFERENCES

INDEX

APPENDIX

Conference and Course Staff 1962-1964

I. RESIDENTIAL CONFERENCES

Leicester/Tavistock 1962-1964; and Tavistock 1964

*A. J. Allaway, M.A., J.P.	University of Leicester
P. W. de Berker, B.Litt., Dip.Psych.	H.M. Prison Commission †
N. A. Bishop	H.M. Prison Commission †
Eileen M. Churchill, M.A.	University of Leicester
R. Gosling, B.Sc., M.D., D.P.M.	Tavistock Clinic and Institute
Marion Mackenzie, M.B., B.S.	Tavistock Clinic
Isabel E. P. Menzies, M.A.	Tavistock Institute
W. Pappenheim, B.A., M.B., B.Ch., B.A.O., D.P.M.	Tavistock Clinic
*A. K. Rice, M.A., Sc.D.	Tavistock Institute
J. Elizabeth Richardson, M.A.	University of Bristol
C. Sofer, M.Sc., Ph.D.	University of Cambridge
J. D. Sutherland, F.R.C.P.E., Ph.D., D.P.M.	Tavistock Clinic
*J. W. Tibble, M.A., M.Ed.	University of Leicester
E. A. Towndrow	H.M. Prison Commission †
*P. M. Turquet, M.A., M.R.C.S., L.R.C.P., D.P.M.	Tavistock Clinic and Institute

Pauline Andrews	Tavistock Institute
Daphne J. Bostock (*Conference Secretary*)	Tavistock Institute
Jean Farquhar (*Joint Conference Secretary*)	University of Leicester
Shirley Mackness	University of Leicester
Margaret Pavitt	Tavistock Institute
Angela Weston	University of Leicester

* Members of Leicester/Tavistock Executive Committee.
† Now the Prison Department of the Home Office.

Christian Teamwork/Tavistock 1963-1964

A. J. Allaway, M.A., J.P.	University of Leicester
R. W. Herrick, B.A.	Canon, Diocese of Chelmsford
B. Reed, M.A., Th.L.	Christian Teamwork
A. K. Rice, M.A., Sc.D.	Tavistock Institute
P. M. Turquet, M.A., M.R.C.S., L.R.C.P., D.P.M.	Tavistock Clinic and Institute
Jean Hutton (*Conference Secretary*)	Christian Teamwork

II. NON-RESIDENTIAL COURSES

W. R. Bion, D.S.O., B.A., M.R.C.S., L.R.C.P.	British Psycho-Analytical Society
R. Gosling, B.Sc., M.D., D.P.M.	Tavistock Clinic and Institute
J. M. M. Hill, M.A.	Tavistock Institute
Marie Jahoda, Ph.D.	Brunel College of Technology
Pearl M. King, B.A.	Tavistock Institute
Isabel E. P. Menzies, M.A.	Tavistock Institute
E. J. Miller, M.A., Ph.D.	Tavistock Institute
A. K. Rice, M.A., Sc.D.	Tavistock Institute
C. Sofer, M.Sc., Ph.D.	University of Cambridge
J. D. Sutherland, F.R.C.P.E., Ph.D., D.P.M.	Tavistock Clinic
P. M. Turquet, M.A., M.R.C.S., L.R.C.P., D.P.M.	Tavistock Institute and Clinic
Daphne J. Bostock (*Course Secretary*)	Tavistock Institute

References

ALLAWAY, A. J. (1959). Introduction to *Exploration in group relations*. Leicester: Leicester University Press.

ARGYRIS, C. (1962). *Interpersonal competence and organizational effectiveness*. Homewood, Illinois: Dorsey Press; London: Tavistock Publications.

BENNIS, W. G. (1959). Leadership theory and administrative behaviour. *Admin. Sci. Quarterly* **4**, 259-301.

BION, W. R. (1961). *Experiences in groups*. London: Tavistock Publications.

BRADFORD, L. P. & GIBB, J. R. (Eds.) (1964). *Theories of T-group training*. New York: Wiley.

BURKE, R. L. & BENNIS, W. G. (1961). Changes in perception of self and others during human relations training. *Hum. Relat.* **14**, 165-82.

FICHELET, R., MEIGNIER, R., MICHELAT, G. & YAUN, L. F. (1963). Comments about an intervention on real environment. Milan: Third International Conference on Group Psychotherapy.

GOSLING, R. & TURQUET, P. (1964). The training of general practitioners: the use of the group method. Paper at conference on group methods. London: Tavistock Institute of Human Relations.

HIGGIN, G. W. & BRIDGER, H. (1964). The psychodynamics of an intergroup experience. *Hum. Relat.* **17**, 391-446. And as Tavistock Pamphlet No. 10. London: Tavistock Publications, 1965.

JAMES, WILLIAM (1890). *The principles of psychology*. London: Macmillan; New York: Holt.

MCGREGOR, D. (1960). *The human side of enterprise*. New York: McGraw-Hill.

MAYO, ELTON (1945). *The social problems of an industrial civilization*. Cambridge, Mass.: Harvard University Press; London: Routledge & Kegan Paul, 1949.

NATIONAL TRAINING LABORATORY (1953). *Human relations training: assessment of experience, 1947-1953*. Washington: National Education Association.

RICE, A. K. (1951). The use of unrecognized cultural mechanisms in an expanding machine shop. *Hum. Relat.* **4**, 143-60.

RICE, A. K. (1963). *The enterprise and its environment*. London: Tavistock Publications.

REFERENCES

RICE, A. K. & TRIST, E. L. (1952). Institutional and sub-institutional determinants of change in labour turnover. *Hum. Relat.* **5**, 347-71.

RICHARDSON, J. E. (1963). Teacher-pupil relationships as explored and rehearsed in an experimental tutorial group. Parts I and II. *New Era* **44**, 134-44 and 166-71.

RICKMAN, J. (1951). Methodology and research in psychological pathology. *Brit. J. med. Psychol.* **24**, Part 1, pp. 1-7.

SELZNICK, P. (1957). *Leadership in administration.* Evanston, Illinois: Row, Peterson.

SOFER, C. (1961). *The organization from within.* London: Tavistock Publications; Chicago, Illinois: Quadrangle.

SUTHERLAND, J. D. (1959). Appendix to *Exploration in group relations.* Leicester: Leicester University Press.

TANNENBAUM, R., WESCHLER, I. R. & MASSARIK, F. (1961). *Leadership and organization: a behavioral science approach.* New York: McGraw-Hill.

TRIST, E. L. & SOFER, C. (1959). *Explorations in group relations.* Leicester: Leicester University Press.

WESCHLER, I. R. & SCHEIN, E. H. (Eds.) (1962). *Issues in training.* Washington: National Education Association.

Index

INDEX